PRAISE FOR JAI

"I needed advice before I tried to write a novel. The usual axiom — write what you know — wasn't helpful. So I turned to James Scott Bell. He taught me how to structure a great entrance — the equivalent of gliding down a spiral staircase in a wedding gown — and how to keep the next 400 pages from becoming as hopelessly tangled as the crumpled papers and wads of gum in my old desk. My novel sold."

— SARAH PEKKANEN, AUTHOR OF THE OPPOSITE OF ME

"James Scott Bell is a master of writing craft with the rare ability to teach others, through his books and workshops. Rather than framing writing ability as gift bestowed upon a chosen few, Jim makes it accessible to anyone who is willing to dig deep and put in the time to learn the craft. I have learned more from Jim's books than any writing course, and this book is no exception. As a former teacher turned novelist, I know how to spot a talented teacher when I see one. James Scott Bell doesn't just make the cut, he sets the standard."

— KAMI GARCIA, #1 NEW YORK TIMES BESTSELLING AUTHOR

"Time well spent. I expect Jim's teaching to inform my writing for years."

— JERRY B. JENKINS, #1 NEW YORK TIMES BESTSELLING AUTHOR

"James Scott Bell is my go-to writing guru!"

— TERRI BLACKSTOCK, NEW YORK TIMES BESTSELLING AUTHOR

"I am inspired by Bell's enthusiastic approach, and impressed with his numerous, helpful insights into the craft of storytelling."

— BILL MARSILII, SCREENWRITER

THE LAST FIFTY PAGES

The Art and Craft of Unforgettable Endings

JAMES SCOTT BELL

Print version:

ISBN 10: 0-910355-43-6

ISBN 13: 978-0-910355-43-8

Cover design by Josh Kenfield.

Published by
Compendium Press
Woodland Hills, CA

CONTENTS

"The first page sells that book. The last page sells your next book."

— Mickey Spillane

1

ENDINGS ARE HARD

There's an old golf saying: "It's not how you drive, it's how you arrive." In other words, no matter how long you hit the ball off the tee, it will make no difference to your overall score unless you can sink some dang putts! Three, four, five tries to get it into the cup? That way lies madness, broken clubs, and too many martinis in the clubhouse.

In the same way, you can write a killer opening scene with dynamic characters and lots of action. You might even sustain that through most of the book.

But if don't sink the putt—if your ending is a letdown—it tarnishes all the good stuff that came before.

And supremely frustrates your readers.

As Exhibit A, I give you the television series *Lost.*

I recall watching most of the first season. It became clear to me how the writers were compelling viewers to tune in each week. They would come up with an inexplicable cliffhanger at the end of an episode, something so surprising it would knock your figurative socks off.

The country was littered with figurative socks as *Lost* became a smash hit.

But I was thinking this: *Do the writers know how this is going to end? Are they going to be able to wrap up all these earth-shattering mysteries?*

After six seasons, the day of reckoning came.

I tracked Twitter on the night of the last episode. The response was mostly negative, running the gamut from confusion to outrage.

Then the blogs began. Some purported to explain what was inexplicable. Others gave vent to the frustration of having watched for six seasons, only to be disappointed at the end. A lot of heat was expended in comments and across platforms, with no settled answers.

Now, I do not entirely blame the writers for what happened. They were writing from episode to episode and putting in fantastic twists, as ordered by the producers. This delighted viewers, network execs, and advertisers alike.

But (he says with italicized emphasis) *coming up with twisty cliffhangers is the easy part!* It's not difficult *at all* to come up with a shocking twist at the end of an episode (or scene in your book) *if you don't worry about having to justify it.*

Which the *Lost* writers found out the hard way.

(Side note: Some time after the series ended, leaked documents and private conversations with the writers revealed this is exactly how *Lost* went down. One of the writers was asked by his friend Nick Santora, a writer on the television series *Prison Break*, "How are you going to pay all this stuff off?" And the writer reportedly answered, "We're not. We literally just think of the weirdest most f****** up thing and write it and we're never going to pay it off." Santora replied in rather colorful language that such a stratagem was, well, let's just say, *not good.*)

Most loyal viewers of *Lost* that I've personally talked to said they loved watching the series but had to admit disappointment at the end.

So here is my wish for you: I want your readers to be so blown away by your endings that they immediately go shopping for more of your books.

A high bar?

Indeed. And it should be. Because people who spend money to buy stories are taking a risk. They want to be swept away in a fictive dream and dropped back into reality only after an ending that leaves them, in some fashion, emotionally satisfied and supremely happy that they gave your novel the time it took to read it.

There's an old acting quote that's been variously attributed, usually to the English actor Edmund Kean (1787 - 1833). He was on his deathbed when a friend remarked how hard this must be. Kean supposedly answered, "Dying is easy. Comedy is hard."

Well, beginnings are easy. Endings are hard.

But when they work—magic.

2

WHAT SHOULD AN ENDING DO?

If there's one word that sums up the feeling readers crave in an ending, it's *satisfaction.* The word is broad enough to include any type of ending, so long as it is one that leaves the reader in a positive emotional state about the reading experience as a whole. Note: this positivity does not only refer to the feeling one gets after a "happy" ending. It also means that the ending feels right for *that* story.

A novel with a downbeat ending—e.g., where the Lead dies, as in a tragedy—can feel right even though you wanted the guy to make it. Like in *Hamlet.*

On the other hand, a happy ending does not always satisfy. There's got to be a sense that the happiness was earned by the characters, not dropped in their laps out of the blue (the *deus ex machina* trap, which we'll discuss in a later chapter).

Why do readers want a satisfying ending?

First, because they often don't get satisfaction in life. They get fired, rear-ended on the highway, have a lousy steak at an expensive restaurant. Then there are the greater tragedies, like the loss of a loved one. The list goes on. Life is relentless.

So when they read a book and get lost in a story, they are hoping that the ending will, in some way, make them glad they held on right through to the finish.

Books, theater, movies, music, dance. When these have a feeling of completeness, they impart a degree of comfort.

The other reason readers want a satisfying ending is less psychological and more practical—they paid money! If the ending isn't up to snuff (as my grandfather used to say), then the reader feels a bit cheated. Or, in the case of a $35 hardcover, a lot cheated.

Here is my friend and blogmate, the bestselling thriller writer John Gilstrap, writing at our group blog Kill Zone (May 24, 2017):

> I just finished a book that was sent to me in search of a blurb. It was one of the most thrilling thrillers I've read in a long time, and because the publisher was on tight time constraints, I gave the book a rave blurb when I was only about three-quarters of the way through. I mean, this was a pulse-pounder.
>
> Until the last 30 pages.
>
> "Before you kill me, you've got to tell me why you did it, and how all of your compatriots fit into the puzzle." Okay, it wasn't that on-the-nose, but it was close. Such a disappointment. I don't regret the blurb, and I would read the author again because of the exciting 9/10 of the storytelling, but I really felt let down. And no, I won't share the book title or the author because I don't think that would be fair.
>
> Folks, this show-don't-tell trope holds from the

> beginning of a story all the way through to the last page. I think that writers sometimes get tired of their own stories, or they're leaning face-first into the fan blades of a submission deadline and they sort of eject from the plot and characters, settling for, "Well, it's good enough."
>
> And you know what? I get that. I'll readily forgive that of an author I've followed and whose works I enjoy, provided it's a one-off. I'll write it off as their Mulligan book, their bye. But at that point, they're on notice. The next book better be up to standard, or they lose their spot on the TBR pile.
>
> This is why the bar is set especially high for new writers. Rookies don't get a Mulligan on their first swing. They've got to slam that baby three hundred yards straight down the fairway.

And, I would add, sink the putt.

Enough with the sports analogies!

No, wait. One more.

The golfer always knows where the green is when he tees off. It would make no sense to hit the ball any which way, now would it?

Thus, the question: should a writer know the ending before setting off to write?

We'll answer that not via the sporting life. We'll go right to the top. We'll ask God.

3

SHOULD YOU KNOW YOUR ENDING BEFORE YOU WRITE?

God was not pleased.

The special creation he had lovingly shaped, and into which he breathed the breath of life, had gone off the rails. *God saw that the wickedness of man was great in the earth, and that every imagination of the thoughts of his heart was only evil continually.*

Things went south from the very start. He placed man and woman in this beautiful garden with plants and animals and a Starbucks, and said there was only one rule: Do not eat the fruit of this certain tree, okay? Is there any part of *Do not eat* you don't understand? No? That is very good.

But then ~~the first politician~~ the serpent whispered a sweet lie, and Eve took a bite. Then Adam chomped, and it was bye-bye Eden.

In the outside world Adam and Eve scraped up enough to buy a little starter cave, had kids, started mowing the lawn.

But tragedy ensued. Cain murdered his brother, Abel.

Things only got worse.

After several generations, God decided it was time to

clear the table, wrap it all up. But there was this one man, Noah, *who was perfect in his generations, and … walked with God.*

You know the story. God tells Noah that judgment is coming, so he is to build an ark according to certain specs. Then he must bring in pairs of animals for the repopulation project. Noah obeys, gets the animals and his family on board. The flood arrives.

And Noah becomes the greatest financial planner in the Bible. He floated his stock while everyone else was liquidated.

Ba-dump-bump.

So there is Noah, inside a stinky animal pen for over a year, and what is he thinking? We have a clue. The ancient Hebrew style of writing is minimalist and leaves a lot "between the lines." At one point we read this: *And God remembered Noah.*

This tells us that sometime during his voyage Noah began to wonder if God had forgotten him. Was he a sap for listening? Was this all a cosmic joke? Was he going to die out here in this watery wasteland?

What Noah experienced was his "Mirror Moment" (which I explain below).

Yet he keeps the faith, does not curse God. The flood subsides. Noah and his family and the animals step out into the new world.

And Noah builded an altar unto the LORD; and took of every clean beast, and of every clean fowl, and offered burnt offerings on the altar. And the LORD smelled a sweet savour …

Noah is the same righteous man he was before the flood, but now his faith has been tested, and he has become stronger.

This is Noah's arc.

Thank you. I'll be here all week.

Arc as Ending Indicator

Some time ago Pixar story artist Emma Coats tweeted a series of "story basics" that guide the team. Their #7 was intriguing: *Come up with your ending before you figure out your middle. Seriously. Endings are hard, get yours working up front.*

This philosophy is 180 degrees from the practice of one Stephen King, as described in his bestselling book *On Writing.* "The situation comes first," he writes. "The characters—always flat and unfeatured, to begin with—come next. Once these things are fixed in my mind, I begin to narrate."

King wants his characters to surprise him, which means he often doesn't know where he's headed. "And why worry about the ending anyway? Why be such a control freak? Sooner or later every story comes out *somewhere.*"

To which a writer might answer, "But suppose, Mr. King, there is no *there* there in the somewhere?"

"Then rewrite the thing," he might say.

"But maybe I could have saved a lot of grief doing it the Pixar way."

"If you wanted to avoid grief, why on earth did you become a writer?"

And so it goes.

There are plotters and pantsers. There are outliners and wingers. There are those who want to know the ending they're writing toward, and those who want it open-ended so the story can guide them (these types will often say, in the whispered assurances of the spiritually enlightened, "Listen to the story. The story always knows.")

Well, I'm not sure anyone or anything, including story, knows *everything.* Sometimes a story can lead you to the edge of a cliff and say, "Well, are you going to jump, or do I have to push you?"

Ray Bradbury famously described writing that way. You jump off a cliff and grow your wings on the way down.

Sometimes that may work.

Sometimes, though, you land like Wile E. Coyote, in a puff of dirt.

My first piece of advice to you is this: have an ending in mind to write *toward.* You can always change it along the way, or when you revise. And the way you come up with an ending is to *start in the middle.*

Because this is where you discover what your story is really all about.

I wrote an entire book on this subject called *Write Your Novel From The Middle.* Here, in brief, is what it's about.

Every story must have a character arc—or as I prefer to call it, a *transformation*—because, wait for it, *you can't have a story without one.* You can have writing. You can have style. You can have quirks. You can have an experiment. But, writer friend, you will not have a story, and that's what 99.9% of readers are looking for.

Which means you can't write a good ending without the arc.

In the very middle of the story, then, the Lead character should have a moment when he is forced to look at himself, as if in a mirror. I call this the Mirror Moment.

There are two types.

The first is where a character is forced to look inside, at himself, and what sort of human being he is at this point in the story. He sees "reflected" back at him a self that is morally flawed.

The other kind of Mirror Moment is one where the character does not look at his moral failings. In fact, he remains basically the same person. It's just that in the middle of the plot he realizes he's probably going to die! The odds (be they physical or professional or psychological) are just too great against him.

So what I say to writers is that your Mirror Moment tells you *what kind of transformation you have.* It also will be one of two types:

1. The Lead character changes inside, becoming a different person at the end than at the beginning. In this type of Mirror Moment, the character is forced to look at himself and "ask" if this is who he really is, and wonder if he's going to stay that way. The story question then is: will he actually transform into a different person at the end?

This is the type of transformation we see in *Casablanca.* In the dead center of the movie, Rick Blaine is drunk in his saloon, after hours. Ilsa, his lost love, comes to him to explain why she had to leave him in Paris. She pours out her heart. Rick pours out his cruelty. He basically calls her a whore. She looks at him with tears in her eyes, thinking, This is not the man I loved. Not anymore.

She leaves. And (visually) Rick puts his head in his hands, knowing what a louse he really is.

Will he stay that way? The final transformation at the end tells us.

That Mirror Moment tells us what *Casablanca* is really about—personal transformation, into the person he's supposed to be, a better self. (If he resists that transformation, we'd have a tragedy.)

Note: This transformation does not have to travel from negative to positive (though most of the time it does). It can also be from positive to negative. A prime example of this is Michael Corleone in *The Godfather.* He transforms from good American soldier to soulless gangster. His Mirror Moment comes when he decides he is going to be the one to kill the traitor Solozzo. There is even a type of transformation where the character is "offered grace" (as Flannery O'Connor put it) but turns it down. This is a *tragedy.* Two of my favorite films of all time, both starring Paul Newman, are examples of this—*Hud* and *The Hustler.*

2. The Lead character realizes, right in the middle of the struggle, that there is no way he can win. The odds are too great. He is "probably going to die."

This transformation goes from *stasis to strength.* The character remains the same person fundamentally, but grows stronger in order to survive the "death stakes" of the conflict.

Examples of this type are: Clarice Starling in *The Silence of the Lambs;* Katniss Everdeen in *The Hunger Games;* Dr. Richard Kimble in *The Fugitive.*

In the middle of *The Fugitive,* Kimble is hiding out in a rented basement in Chicago. He's trying to figure out how to get into Cook County hospital without being noticed, so he can get access to the prosthetics records (which could lead him to the one-armed man who murdered his wife).

Suddenly, cops surround the house! And start yelling!

Kimble is trapped, he doesn't know which way to go!

But it turns out they are not there for Kimble, but for the drug-dealing son of the woman who owns the place.

Realizing this, after the adrenaline overload, Kimble

breaks down. He's thinking, *I can't possibly survive. I can't fight against all this. I'm going to die.*

That's the essence of this second type of Mirror Moment. The character thinking along the lines of what Katniss thinks in the middle of *The Hunger Games: This is an okay place to die, I think.*

Are there any examples of characters without any type of Mirror Moment or transformation? What about James Bond? Jack Reacher? They're always the same, aren't they?

They are the same fundamentally, but in those stories the transformation is of the second type, because *the case or intrigue they are involved in challenges their powers and threatens them with physical, professional or psychological death.*

If the story doesn't have death on the line, it's going to feel flat.

The easiest way to find the transformation that is right for your story is to brainstorm your Mirror Moment.

Pantsers, you can brainstorm that anytime you like. If you're lost in the middle of a draft (and I know you will be), the Mirror Moment will become the beacon that lights your way out of the thicket.

Plotters, you can determine your transformation at the beginning of things and know precisely how to outline from there (in my book I describe the "Golden Triangle" as the basis of a solid outline). Or you can put a moment in provisionally and change it later on as the story grows.

The point is that once you have it, it will illuminate the rest of your novel, from beginning to end. It will guide you in the formulation of plot, scenes and the ultimate meaning (theme) of the story trying to get out.

And move you toward an unforgettable ending.

4

ABOUT ACT 3

I'm a three-act structure guy, and make no apologies about it.

Even those who claim there's no such thing as the three-act structure end up, in their fiction or their teaching, being three-act structure guys.

It's just that instead of calling it beginning, middle, and end, they'll make up some other terms for it, like: origination, escalation, and resolution.

Even the famous screenwriting guru who cursed out another famous screenwriting guru for suggesting there is a three-act template for movies, ended up laying out all these beats that, gasp, fell into three acts.

Because *that's how people are wired to receive stories.*

Sure, you can play around with structure. You can even ignore it and write what's called "experimental fiction" (which is also called "fiction that doesn't sell"). You're free.

Just know that to create an unforgettable ending you need to lay the right foundation. I've never found any foundation as strong as the three-act structure.

This is not a book covering the intricacies of the three

acts. I've done that in another book, *Super Structure.* Instead, I'll reiterate my basic plot development summary, called the LOCK System.

L stands for Lead. The protagonist.

O is Objective, what the Lead must get (or get away from). This objective must be in the form of a life-or-death struggle. There are three kinds of death: physical, professional, or psychological.

C is Confrontation. The Lead must be opposed by a force—embodied in another character or group—that is stronger than the Lead.

K is for Knock-Out Ending, which is the subject of this book. For that reason, let's look a bit more deeply at what is happening in Act 3.

We are moving toward the climax, where the plot will be resolved—an ending organically related to the previous acts.

In Act 1 we were introduced to the Lead. We read to follow this character if he or she is ready to demonstrate strength-of-will. At the end of Act 1, the Lead was pushed through a Doorway of No Return, right into the confrontations of Act 2.

When I say "pushed," that's what it's got to feel like. Because Act 2, remember, is about one of the three forms of death. If the stakes are not that high, the book is not going to be gripping. The Lead (like all of us) doesn't want to have to face death. We would rather stay in our ordinary world, nice and comfy.

But that won't make a novel.

So there is Dorothy Gale, Kansas farm girl, who is unhappy and wants to run away. But convinced by Professor Marvel to go back to the farm because, he tells her, Aunt Em's heart is breaking. But just when she gets there, a twister rolls through and pushes (literally, lifts) Dorothy into Act 2. (Hint: When a movie changes from black and white to color, you've probably moved to Act 2).

Or Scarlett O'Hara, the coquette. She wants to stay in the Old South and marry Ashley Wilkes and wear big-hoop dresses and throw parties. But the Civil War forces her through a Doorway of No Return.

It's "No Return" because we have to feel that the door slams shut, and locks. The Lead cannot go back. She can only go forward and fight through the plot.

So how do you move from Act 2 into Act 3? Another Doorway of No Return. Because through a clue, discovery, setback, or crisis, the resolution is now possible. Without this Doorway, the Lead would be going on and on through challenge after challenge, but would not be able to end the struggle with death.

Thus:

In *The Fugitive*, Dr. Kimble has managed to break into the apartment of a man with a prosthetic arm. Kimble got prosthetics records by sneaking into Cook County Hospital disguised as a custodian. He's been tracking down those on the list. This guy is the last one.

And what does he find? A major clue. He sees a photo of the man he fought with, the man who killed his wife, alongside a well-known doctor, and near some records showing the one-armed man's employment as security for a big pharmaceutical company.

With this information, Kimble is able to make a beeline toward the resolution of the mystery.

Dorothy Gale is captured by the Wicked Witch's flying monkeys. That happens at the 3/4 mark of *The Wizard of Oz*. It is a major setback. It requires the three allies—the scarecrow, the tin man, and the lion—to break into the castle to save her. Which leads to the final confrontation with the witch.

So we pass through the Doorway of No Return #2, because there's no going back. The Lead has to go forward in order to gain the victory.

The scenes I like to see in Act 3 are:

Mounting Forces

The antagonist—knowing the battle is really on and that the Lead is committed—mounts larger forces to defeat the Lead.

Lights Out

When it looks like all is lost for the Lead. There's no way to win!

Note: The last fifty pages will start around this point, though it's flexible depending on the type of book you're writing, and the length. In any event, the Final Battle is now on the horizon. The Lead should be experiencing some fear or doubt. It is going to take an act of courage to fight to the finish. That's why we need:

Q Factor

The Q Factor is an emotional jolt that gives the Lead the courage to fight on or make the right choice, by recalling or seeing something of emotional impact from Act I, or hearing from a trusted character about the need to fight or choose rightly. Luke Skywalker hears the voice of Obi Wan Kenobi:

"Use The Force." Or when Mr. Smith, in *Mr. Smith Goes to Washington,* is about to pack it in and leave town. But then Saunders, the female aide who has fallen for him, finds him sitting at the Lincoln Memorial. She reminds Smith of what he said when he first arrived and (in Act 1) visited the memorial. He'd said that Mr. Lincoln looked like he was waiting for the right person to come along. She tells Smith he's that person. When Smith looks again at the monument, he's inspired all over again.

Final Battle

Outer (will Lead overcome the forces?) and/or Inner (will Lead make the right choice?). This is the big, climactic scene or sequence, the fictive spot with all the chips in the middle of the table. To fight this battle he is going to need guts—either a raw act of physical courage, as displayed by Luke Skywalker in the attack on the Death Star; or a raw act of moral courage, as Rick demonstrates in *Casablanca.* In a downbeat ending (discussed in the next chapter) we flip these on their head. For example, in *The Godfather,* Michael lacks the moral courage to turn his back on a life of crime.

Transformation

Usually the last chapter of the book, *showing* us the character's change to stronger self or new self, and carrying the emotional resonance you want to leave with the audience. This matter of resonance is so important I give it a chapter of its own.

In the next chapter, we'll look at some examples so you can see these scenes in action. Meanwhile…

Try This:

Watch a few classic movies and try to identify the Act 3 beats as explained above. Then brainstorm each one of these for your own Act 3. Come up with two, three, or four possibilities for each beat. Think outside the box. Choose the best options and adjust your plot as needed.

Reject the most obvious choices. What you want are things that surprise the reader but which, upon reflection, seems inevitable. You then go back inside your novel and plant what you need in order to justify the actions. Not an easy task, which is why endings are hard. But this hard work will pay big dividends, the primary one being the transformation of readers into fans.

5

THE SHAPE OF YOUR ENDING

The Lead in a novel has an objective. He battles with strength-of-will to gain that objective. The outcome of this battle determines the shape of the ending, of which there are five:

1. The Lead wins
2. The Lead loses
3. The Lead sacrifices
4. The Lead "wins" but really loses
5. Open-ended

Let's take a look at each.

1. The Lead Wins

Boy meets girl. Boy tries to win girl's love. Girl's family is against boy. Boy becomes a better man and ends up with the girl.

He's won. He has gained the objective.

Detective gets case. Lots of stuff happens. At the end the killer is nabbed.

Detective has won.

Woman has awful childhood. Her mother tries to destroy her self-image. Woman is loved by a man who enables her to come into her own. She stands up to her mother, who has a heart attack and dies.

Woman has won the battle to become her own person, and even though she is somewhat sad her mother bought the farm, it's a victory. (See the classic Bette Davis movie *Now, Voyager.*)

A victory in a novel must never be easy. It must cost something. The Lead usually suffers a wound (internal or external) that will leave a scar but also makes him stronger, better. In the beginning of *The Fugitive,* Dr. Richard Kimble suffers a deep, physical wound in the side in order to escape the prison bus (external). At the end he suffers the wound of betrayal by a trusted friend (internal).

In a Lead Wins novel, the battle is fierce—as it should be in all fiction—but we can firmly state at the end that the Lead has gained his objective.

As in the first book of Don Pendleton's wildly successful vigilante series, *The Executioner.* Subtitled *War Against the Mafia,* it's the story of Mack Bolan, Viet Nam vet and master sniper, who returns home only to find that mob loan sharks are responsible for the grisly deaths of his father, mother and teen-aged sister. Bolan declares war and begins a one-man execution run, utilizing his skills to take out one wise guy after another. Not only is the Mafia after Bolan, so are the cops, who can't have this guy running around shooting things up.

It all culminates in a big battle in the town of Pittsfield. Which Mack Bolan wins:

> The battle of Pittsfield had ended. Victory, for Mack Bolan, had been not an era but a miniscule point in time which had already receded into the fuzzy past, one that was absorbed and neutralized by the perilous present and which stood under the constant threat of being reversed.

But Bolan knows there is a cost to his new life:

> There was nothing ahead but hell. He was prepared for hell. Somebody else, he avowed, had better get prepared for it, too. Mack Bolan's last mile would be a bloody one. The Executioner was going to live life to the very end.

And brother, that life still hasn't ended. As of this writing, there have been 460 installments!

To give us a little softer side of the Lead Wins ending, let's consider the romance genre. In many lines it is required to have a happily-ever-after (HEA) ending. That is, both lovers get what they want at the end—each other.

Perhaps the most famous of these is Jane Austen's *Pride and Prejudice.* Elizabeth and Darcy end up together at last, even winning over Darcy's hostile aunt:

> Lady Catherine was extremely indignant on the marriage of her nephew; and as she gave way to all the genuine frankness of her character in her reply to the letter which announced its arrangement, she sent him language so very abusive, especially of Elizabeth, that for some time all intercourse was at an end. But at length, by Elizabeth's persuasion, he was prevailed on to overlook the offence, and seek a reconciliation; and, after a little further resistance on the part of his aunt, her resentment gave way,

> either to her affection for him, or her curiosity to see how his wife conducted herself; and she condescended to wait on them at Pemberley, in spite of that pollution which its woods had received, not merely from the presence of such a mistress, but the visits of her uncle and aunt from the city.
>
> With the Gardiners, they were always on the most intimate terms. Darcy, as well as Elizabeth, really loved them; and they were both ever sensible of the warmest gratitude towards the persons who, by bringing her into Derbyshire, had been the means of uniting them.

Is there a wound here? As the title suggests, both pride and prejudice need to be cut out of the main characters. That operation leaves a mark, but not one so egregious that it cannot be overcome. As Elizabeth tells her sister: "Perhaps I did not always love him so well as I do now. But in such cases as these, a good memory is unpardonable. This is the last time I shall ever remember it myself."

So remember the shape of the Lead Wins ending:

- Death stakes (physical, professional, or psychological) in the final battle.
- The Lead wins by gaining the objective (defeating an enemy; gaining love, etc.)
- The victory leaves some sort of wound—internal, external, or both.

2. The Lead Loses

When a Lead character fails in his quest, you have what is known as a *downbeat* ending. In a classic tragedy, the hero dies or is punished because of his *tragic flaw*. Hamlet dies because he is blinded by revenge. King Lear dies because of pride and anger. Macbeth is done in by ambition.

A famous Lead Loses novel is F. Scott Fitzgerald's *The Great Gatsby*.

Narrated by the character Nick Carraway, it is the story of a wealthy but mysterious character named Jay Gatsby, who throws wild parties at his mansion during the Roaring 20s. Gatsby befriends Nick, and we soon know why. Living nearby is Daisy Buchanan, Nick's cousin, and the object of Jay Gatsby's obsessive love. Though she is married to another man, Gatsby has come to town in order to win Daisy back.

He almost does, but Daisy decides to stay with her husband, Tom Buchanan. Her driving, however, stinks, and she runs down and kills a character named Myrtle with Gatsby's car. Gatsby is willing to take the blame, but Myrtle's husband thinks Gatsby was having an affair with Myrtle (it was really Tom). So George goes to Gatsby's and shoots him dead before turning the gun on himself.

So not only does Gatsby fail to win Daisy back, he ends up pushing up daisies forever.

What purpose does a downbeat ending serve?

For Fitzgerald, it had to do with a critique of the American dream—which usually revolves around money, and a lot of it—and the inability to recapture the past.

That's how a downbeat ending can carry with it a moral message. Gatsby's demise was caused by his going after the wrong things, such as massive wealth (through bootlegging) and another man's wife. He paid for it.

And in doing so, Fitzgerald awakens us to the futility of the same pursuits.

Tragedy and Catharsis

In classic Greek drama, the tragedy served to create what Aristotle called *catharsis,* meaning purification or cleansing. While academics get doctorates unpacking what Aristotle meant, it seems to me the object was to get the audience to avoid destructive passions, thus strengthening the state for survival. Professor Rufus Fears put it this way in an essay on the Greek tragedy *Alcestis:*

> The purpose of . . . tragedy was to awaken in you the emotions of fear and pity and, thereby, to achieve a catharsis—a purging of those emotions, as when you eat too many prunes—to cleanse you so you could then, without fear and pity, make decisions. (Fears, J. Rufus, *Life Lessons from the Great Books,* The Great Courses, 2009).

A downbeat ending should operate in a similar way. We feel relieved that we do not suffer the fate of the Lead. And are "warned" in a way so that we can avoid the same demise. Ray Bradbury, author of the dystopian classic *Fahrenheit 451*, was once asked why he wrote stories that predicted the future. He replied, "I don't try to predict the future. I try to prevent it."

This Lead Loses ending is common in classic film noir and hardboiled fiction.

Think of the doomed lovers in James M. Cain's *Double Indemnity* and *The Postman Always Rings Twice.* In both plots the question is, Will they get away with murder?

And let's face it, there is a part of us—the part that needs the warning—that in some way hopes they do get away with it. Why? Because Cain is able to create sympathy for them.

This creates cross-currents of emotion which is one of the hallmarks of better-than-average fiction.

As *Postman* draws to a close, the lovers, Frank and Cora, seal their love, in part because Cora is now pregnant.

> We got married at the City Hall, and then we went to the beach. She looked so pretty I just wanted to play in the sand with her, but she had this little smile on her face, and after a while she got up and went down to the surf.
>
> "I'm going out."
>
> She went ahead, and I swam after her. She kept on going, and went a lot further out than she had before. Then she stopped, and I caught up with her. She swung up beside me, and took hold of my hand, and we looked at each other. She knew, then, that the devil was gone, that I loved her.

But fate has other ideas. Worrying about a possible miscarriage, Frank drives hard toward a hospital, but when he tries to pass a truck he hits a wall and everything goes black.

> When I came out of it I was wedged down beside the wheel, with my back to the front of the car, but I began to moan from the awfulness of what I heard. It was like rain on a tin roof, but that wasn't it. It was her blood, pouring down on the hood, where she went through the windshield. Horns were blowing, and people were jumping out of cars and running to her. I got her up, and tried to stop the blood and in between I was talking to her, and crying, and kissing her. Those kisses never reached her. She was dead.

Frank is put on trial for faking an accident to murder Cora, so he could have all the money they'd absconded with. He's convicted and sent to the death house. The book ends thus:

> Here they come. Father McConnell says prayers help. If you've got this far, send up one for me, and Cora, and make it that we're together, wherever it is.

So a downbeat ending, where the Lead loses everything, often is based upon a rough but inevitable justice. Which is why they can be among the most powerful endings in literature.

The shape of a Lead Loses ending:

- Death stakes in the final battle.
- The Lead loses, meaning he dies either physically, professionally, or psychologically when he fails to gain his objective.
- A moral lesson is taken away (catharsis).

3. The Lead Sacrifices

What is the most famous ending of all time?

I'll cast my vote for *Casablanca.* It is certainly has one of the great last lines: *Louis, I think this is the beginning of a beautiful friendship.*

Based on a play called *Everybody Comes to Rick's*, *Casablanca* was brought to the screen by Warner Bros. as a vehicle for Humphrey Bogart. (That it was seriously considered for Ronald Reagan is a matter of historical dispute.)

It's the story of Rick Blaine, American, operating a

cafe/saloon in the city of Casablanca during World War II. French Morocco is under the authority of the Nazi-controlled Vichy government. The local police, headed by Captain Louis Renault, allow Rick to conduct his business (which includes a gambling room) because Rick professes absolute neutrality . . . and because Louis gets a kickback from the gambling, and procures desperate women at the cafe for his "little romances" (in return for which he gives the women and their husbands the papers necessary to get out of Casablanca).

Why is Rick such a loner? We don't find out until the past comes back to his present in the form of the one woman he ever truly loved—Ilsa Lund. She's with her husband, the heroic underground fighter, Victor Laszlo.

In a flashback we learn why Rick is so embittered. He and Ilsa had fallen in love in Paris just before the occupation by the Nazis. Ilsa thought that her husband, Laszlo, had died in a concentration camp. She finds out she was wrong, at just the time Rick proposes marriage.

She tells Rick she'll meet him at the train station for the last train out. Instead she writes a note to Rick, telling him she cannot come with him but to know she'll always love him.

Now, here she is, in Casablanca. With the police and the Nazis determined to keep Laszlo from escaping their grasp.

Intrigue happens (that's how to summarize a plot!). But you all know the movie.

Let's analyze.

First, what is this movie all about? It's about the resurrection of a man named Rick Blaine. He goes from embittered isolation to sacrificial hero. Thus, these beats are clear in the movie:

Argument against transformation

In Act 1, Rick says, "I stick my neck out for nobody." He shows this by refusing to step in and help the oily con artist Ugarte from certain execution.

Rick's argument is found in those words. It's not worth ever sticking your neck out for anybody but yourself, results be damned.

Mirror Moment

We discussed this earlier. Rick has a visual moment of self-loathing after drunkenly resisting Ilsa's need to explain what happened in Paris. He knows he's a louse.

The second half of the movie asks, Will Rick recover his humanity?

Foreshadowing the ending

There are moments before Act 3 when Rick shows small signs that he might be moving toward humanity again. Two of them stand out.

One is when the Nazis in the cafe start singing a German song and Victor Laszlo stands up and asks the orchestra to play the free French anthem. The head of the orchestra looks to Rick for a sign of what to do.

Rick nods his okay.

The second incident involves a desperate young woman whose husband is losing all their money in the gambling room, money they need to buy papers to get out. Louis Renault has offered her his normal bargain—sleep with him, and she'll have the papers. Rick arranges for the husband to win at roulette so the wife won't have to go through with it.

Intrigue follows, until at the end Rick is at the airport with Ilsa, who looks remarkably like Ingrid Bergman, and she's ready to leave her husband and go away with him.

But then Rick stops and tells her no, this is wrong. If we go through with it we'll regret it, maybe not now but soon and for the rest of our lives.

And yet: "We'll always have Paris. Here's looking at you, kid."

Rick has sacrificed the thing he wants most in this world. He has done it for a higher good (no longer will he say, "I stick my neck out for nobody.").

He's also put his very life on the line, for he has killed the Nazi major in front of the French police captain, Louis.

But in a stunning reversal, Louis does not arrest Rick. Instead, moved by Rick's moral courage, he himself sacrifices his position of power to go off and fight the Nazis with Rick.

What's happened?

Rick, who has been living as an isolated dead man walking, has offered to sacrifice his life ... and has been resurrected.

The central message of sacrifice and resurrection is the shaping force of our civilization. Even if one is not religious it must be acknowledged that there is something in us that vitally responds to a sacrifice for the greater good.

Which is why *Casablanca* resonates.

And why sacrifice in fiction moves us.

Almost as if we'd been wired to receive it.

In the oldest Hindu text, *Rigveda*, we have the creation story of Purusha, a primal human who, through self-sacrifice (as in, body parts being separated!) became man and woman and, indeed, the stuff of the entire world.

In the Old Testament, Abraham offers Isaac in a test of faith. Isaac is symbolically raised from the dead, pre-figuring Christ, the atoning sacrifice for the whole world.

Four hundred years before Christ, the Athenian playwright Euripides wrote *Alcestis.* In this play a king named Admetus is due to kick the bucket. But he is given a gift by the gods—he does not have to die if he can find someone to take his place.

No one is anxious to step in for that particular service, except his wife, Queen Alcestis. She does this so her children will not be left fatherless and she a grieving widow. Plus, she knows he is a good king and the people need him.

Sacrifice.

Off she goes with Death, toward her eternal destiny.

Meanwhile, Heracles (the Greek name for Hercules, which is the Roman name for Steve Reeves), hears this sad tale and vows to battle Death and bring Alcestis back from the dead.

Which he does. He returns to the palace with a veiled Alcestis. King Admetus doesn't know her at first. But then he lifts her veil and there she is. Interestingly, she cannot speak for three days, and then she is fully restored.

Sacrifice is powerful. Perhaps the reason is this: we know life is tough, and that to stand up for the good usually comes at a cost. Fictional characters who fight for what's right are going to be wounded. Otherwise, the thing they're standing up for isn't all that important.

When they offer their lives, it is the ultimate sacrifice. If they survive, it is like a resurrection.

But even if they do not survive, there is still a resurrection. Their spirit will live on. Their sacrifice inspires others to change for the better and carry on the fight. Think of William Wallace in *Braveheart.* He can end his torture simply by confessing to treason. Instead he shouts, "Freedom!" just before the ax falls. His death inspires his followers, most notably Robert the Bruce, so they may all go on to fight like free men.

Or even the comedy *Mister Roberts.* The novel, play and movie (starring Henry Fonda, Jack Lemmon and James Cagney) were huge successes, in large part because the ending hits us with a somber jolt that is followed by the rebirth of one Ensign Pulver.

We can list other examples. *A Tale of Two Cities* is notable for the self-sacrifice of Sydney Carton, who states, "It is a far, far better thing that I do, than I have ever done; it is a far, far better rest that I go to than I have ever known."

Gran Torino, the film starring Clint Eastwood. He goes from being an entrenched bigot to offering his life to save a Hmong teenager and rid the neighborhood of a vicious gang.

You can see that the sacrificial ending works all over the place, in any type of fiction.

But even if you don't *end* with a sacrifice, at least have the conflict of the novel cost the Lead something essential. He will then emerge as a different or stronger person at the close. That's the essence of story in a nutshell.

The shape of The Lead Sacrifices ending:

- Death stakes that lead to a moral dilemma.
- Lead chooses to sacrifice what he wants most, even his life.
- Lead is rewarded for his sacrifice, with either a

surprising benefit (*Casablanca*) or by saving others and becoming a hero, even in death (*Gran Torino*).

4. The Lead "Wins" But Really Loses

When a Lead goes after an objective that is morally wrong or questionable, and gets it, then technically he's "won." The story question—will he gain the objective?—is answered affirmatively. But there is too great a price to be paid for the victory. Thus, for the Lead, the whole thing turns into a net loss.

Mario Puzo's *The Godfather* is not really about Vito Corleone. Rather, it's the story of Vito's son, Michael, and his rise to power.

At the beginning of the book (and movie), Michael is a returning war veteran. He's come home to marry his fiancé, Kay. At the big wedding of his sister, Connie, he assures Kay that he is not going to be part of the "family business."

But that all changes when a rival, Solozzo, attempts to assassinate Michael's father.

The attempt is unsuccessful, but Vito Corleone is barely hanging onto life. At the hospital, Michael (the smartest of the three brothers) immediately discerns that another assassination attempt is in the offing. His quick thinking frustrates the attempt, but as a result he runs afoul of a corrupt New York police captain. The captain smashes Michael's face.

In the Corleone compound, Sonny, now leading the family, is hot, wants to go to war. Tom Hagen, the family *consigliere*, advises restraint.

All the while, Michael is sitting there, silent. In the movie, this is the Mirror Moment. You can see it visually. Michael is wondering who he is. Is he the good son, the one who told

Kay he's not going to get involved? Or will he take the unalterable step over to the criminal side?

He chooses the latter by coming up with a plan to kill both Solozzo and the police captain.

Once that's done, he goes into hiding in Sicily.

When he returns to New York, it is to take control of the Corleone family and interests.

And to unleash hell on the other families.

His vendetta is a success. He wins.

But at what cost?

At the very end, Michael is confronted by his sister, Connie, who accuses him of ordering the hit on her husband, Carlo. He did, of course. But his wife, Kay, overhears Connie's charge and when they are alone she asks him if it's true.

> Michael shook his head wearily. "Of course it's not. Just believe me, this one time I'm letting you ask about my affairs, and I'm giving you an answer. It is not true." He had never been more convincing. He looked directly into her eyes. He was using all the mutual trust they had built up in their married life to make her believe him. And she could not doubt any longer. She smiled at him ruefully and came into his arms for a kiss.

And so Michael has become the kind of man who can lie, without qualm, to his own wife. His soul is lost. (In the movie, there's a perfect visual image at the end. Kay is standing outside Michael's office and sees Clemenza and some others paying their respects. Clemenza kisses Michael's hand and utters, "Godfather." As he does, a man walks to the door. In the last shot we see Kay's face as the door closes on it.)

The lose-while-winning type of ending is often in horror fiction. This is where you find the Faustian bargain (selling your soul to the devil) and see the cost of dabbling with darkness.

Stephen King's *Pet Sematary*, like much of his fiction, has such an ending. The book concerns Louis Creed, a young doctor with a nice family who moves to a small town in Maine. And because this is a Stephen King town, there's a piece of ground with mysterious powers. That ground is a pet cemetery (the sign is misspelled), and things buried there come back to life as zombie-like reanimations of themselves. Like Louis's cat, which comes back after burial as a mouse-ripping, odoriferous feline.

When Louis's two-year-old son, Gage, is killed by a truck, Louis secretly buries him in the pet cemetery. Big mistake. The kid comes back as a murdering monster. He snags a scalpel and kills Louis's friend, Jud, and then kills his own mother. Not only that, the reanimated tyke has eaten some of her flesh.

Remember, this is Stephen King, not Barbara Cartland.

Louis has to kill his son with a fatal dose of morphine.

Now Louis is teetering on the edge of insanity (ya think?). He takes his wife to the burial ground, reasoning that he'd waited too long with Gage. His wife will come back and be okay!

Yeah, no.

Louis does win the battle over death. But he gets a zombie in return.

Too great a cost.

The shape of this ending:

- The Death at stake is usually psychological death. The Lead is being drawn to the dark side.
- The Lead makes the choice to fully embrace the immoral way (often by refusing the admonition of a character urging him to do what is right, or to stop dealing with darkness.)
- The dark objective is realized, but we see at the end, at the moral cost to the soul.

5. Open-Ended

If a book ends without the main plot being fully resolved, it's called "open-ended." That means it's left to the reader to contemplate what happens after the last line. It will be something in the future, but what? There is more life to come, more character transformation.

This can frustrate a reader, which is why most bestselling fiction is unambiguous about the ending. A definite resolution is usually an implied guarantee in the reading contract. The reader has shelled out time and (usually) discretionary income to experience a story. If they make it all the way through, they're hoping for closure. Bad guy gets his just desserts. Potential lovers end up together. Hero dies, but for a greater good. Crime doesn't pay.

So is there a place for open-ended endings? Of course, but that place is usually in so-called literary fiction. As the noted editor Dave King put it in a Writer Unboxed blog column (4/18/2017):

> But readers of mainstream and literary novels, who often read to experience real life, are a lot more likely to be

> suspicious of an ending that resolves things. The conflicts that infest people's real lives rarely wrap up in nice, satisfying packages. The desire to capture this authentic experience may be why writers of literary novels often shy away from endings that actually end the story. And if the pain your characters go through shows your readers enough about the human condition to leave them thinking, you can sometimes get away without resolving your characters' lives.

This is certainly the case with a novel like J. D. Salinger's *The Catcher in the Rye.* Holden Caulfield, the adolescent in search of a reason to live, is in a sanitarium being treated for depression. At the end of the book he has no idea what life is going to be like when he gets out.

> A lot of people, especially this one psychoanalyst guy they have here, keep asking me if I'm going to apply myself when I go back to school next September. It's such a stupid question, in my opinion. I mean how do you know what you're going to do till you do it? The answer is, you don't. I think I am, but how do I know? I swear it's a stupid question.

And then we're left with the haunting last lines.

> Don't ever tell anybody anything. If you do, you start missing everybody.

Will Holden make it on the outside? That's left up to us. And in this case, I believe the ending works. The book is about experiencing a boy's "real life" struggles. By the time it's over, we'll have our own view of his future. It also helps when you can write a last chapter like Salinger.

But when a book has been plot-centric and does not resolve, the effect is not usually a good one. An example of this (in my opinion) is Elmore Leonard's Western, *Valdez is Coming.*

The plot is straight-forward and compelling. A small-town constable, Bob Valdez, is manipulated by a rancher named Tanner into shooting a black man thought to be a murderer and Army deserter. Only it turns out to be the wrong man. The dead man was married to an Apache woman, who is pregnant. Bob Valdez wants to take up a collection for her.

But when Valdez rides out to Tanner's place to seek a donation, Tanner has his men shame him and send him away. When Valdez tries once again, Tanner has him tortured.

That turns the mild-mannered Valdez into an agent of retribution. He wounds one of Tanner's men and sends the bleeding man back to Tanner with a simple message: *Valdez is coming.*

The plot, then, is a revenge narrative. Tanner is a sadist throughout. He deserves Western justice.

But the book ends without allowing us to see the justice demanded by the plot. (There is one particularly violent scene involving the terrorizing of a family—battery on a young boy, the threat of rape to a young girl, and the burning down of the family's home. If anyone deserves the business end of a Colt .45, it's this man Tanner.)

So with all the emotion that's been built up, we get to the end, with Tanner and Valdez facing each other and. . .the book just ends! It's almost as if Leonard left the last page in his typewriter when he sent in the manuscript.

This, by the way, Leonard himself copped to. In an interview he once quipped, "I have to be satisfied with the ending even though my editor might say, 'This book ends awfully abruptly.' And then I say, 'But it's over.' "

With all due respect (and I mean that) for Leonard's obvious strengths, I'm on that editor's side regarding this ending. After enduring the evil of Tanner for the entire book, I needed to *see* what happens to him.

Now, a critic may argue that *Valdez is Coming* is really an anti-Western, or a post-modern Western, or even a literary Western. Fine.

I call it a Western that didn't end well.

Which is a risk you take with a reader when leaving an ending open like this.

Yet there is a way for genre novel to exploit the literary feel of an open end. If done well, it can elevate—rather than detract from—the reading experience.

The secret is having the openness relate not to the plot, but to the character.

I first became aware of this years ago when I read Dean Koontz's *Midnight.* The plot is a bio-medical horror story, a mix of *The Island of Dr. Moreau* and *Invasion of the Body Snatchers.* The main character is an FBI agent, Sam Booker, who goes to investigate the strange deaths happening in a quiet, seaside town. There's an unforgettable villain and several other well-drawn characters.

Koontz, at this time in his career, was purposely upping his game from straight-ahead genre fiction to more complex characterizations and themes. It worked, as *Midnight* became his first #1 *New York Times* hardcover bestseller.

What Koontz did was create a backstory for Sam Booker involving his troubled teen-age son. Sam is not good at relating to people on a deep personal level. But after going through all the horrific events of the book, and bonding with other characters, he is a changed man. He has the courage now to be a real father.

So after all the plot elements are resolved, Koontz gives us one final scene between father and son. The book ends like this:

> Sam was sure he had not really gotten through the boy's rage. Hadn't more than scratched the surface. Sam had let an evil into their lives, the evil of self-indulgent despair, which he transmitted to the boy, and now rooting it out would be a hard job. They had a long way to go, months of struggle, maybe even years, lots of hugging, lots of holding on tight and not letting go.
>
> Looking over Scott's shoulder, he saw that Tessa and Chrissie had stepped into the room. They were crying too. In their eyes he saw an awareness that matched his, a recognition that the battle for Scott had only begun.
>
> But it *had* begun. That was the wonderful thing. It *had* begun.

You will note that the language of the last line is hopeful. It gives an upward trajectory to the open end. If Koontz had left that last line out, the trajectory would have been neutral. Which means skilled writers can leave a story just where they want in order to achieve the effect they desire.

One last example, perhaps the most famous. Remember this one? A stubborn Southern belle becomes the only one in her family able to save their home in the aftermath of the Civil War. She'll do it, because she wants to live the old life with her great love, Ashley Wilkes, even though she has agreed to marry that rogue Rhett Butler. Then, at the end, she realizes it's Rhett she really loves. But it's too late. He's had it with her, and the tragic loss of their daughter only makes things worse. He no longer gives a damn, and walks out on her. This Southern belle, however, determines she'll find a way to get him back. But she'll think about that tomorrow, for tomorrow is another day.

Will Scarlett get Rhett back?

We don't know the answer. It is left to us as an open-ended question to which we bring our own feelings and desires. (Please don't mention the sequel that was approved of by the Margaret Mitchell estate. Two things you should never do: write a sequel to *Gone With the Wind* and re-make *Casablanca.*)

The shape of the Open Ended Ending:

- Death—professional or psychological—on the line. Physical death is not, because that is a definite ending.
- There is a Final Battle, but the ultimate outcome is not provided.
- However, the author can provide a trajectory.
- A memorable last line is essential.

Whether you outline or not, you ought to at least plan an ending shape. It's not hard to do. No matter how you work, you will have a sense of where you're going—or want to go—with your novel. Choosing a shape to head toward will give focus to your writing. Certainly you can change the shape when you get to the end. But more often than not you'll find your instinct was correct.

Thriller writer John Gilstrap has a popular series

featuring Jonathan Grave, a hostage rescue expert. I once asked John how he outlines his plots. He smiled and said, "Bad guys do something very bad. Jonathan is hired, has a personal stake in the outcome. There's lots of action. Jonathan wins."

That's called knowing the shape of your ending.

6

THE MEANING OF YOUR ENDING

What does your novel ultimately mean? What message will readers take away from it?

And by message I don't mean there has to be some neon sign flashing that says something like *WHAT THE WORLD NEEDS NOW IS LOVE SWEET LOVE!*

That's a nice message and all, and you can certainly hold that one out if you like. But you have to filter it through a real, three-dimensional character in a justified life-and-death struggle.

Agent and writing instructor Donald Maass says: "A breakout novelist believes that what she has to say is not just worth saying, but it is something that must be said. Strong novelists have strong opinions. More to the point, they are not at all afraid to express them." (*Writing the Breakout Novel.*)

However, that expression has to come through a real plot and real characters. You must, at all costs, resist the impulse to stack the deck in favor of your viewpoint. One of the easiest ways to kill a novel is to preach in it.

In *Writing for the Soul*, novelist Jerry B. Jenkins says, "I see this problem in many manuscripts: all talk, straw men, plots contrived to prove a point, but little that grabs and subtly persuades the reader. If your theme is the danger of alcoholism, simply tell a story in which an alcoholic suffers because of his bad decisions, and give the reader credit. Trust me, he'll get it. If your story is powerful enough, your theme will come through."

At some point—whether at the start or the finish or the revision of your novel—you should be able to state the meaning you want the reader to come away with. Even if you're one of those writers who doesn't like "theme" and just writes to entertain, understand that your ending *will* convey a meaning. It therefore helps if you dig it out at some point. Because then you can revise or polish with that meaning in mind.

One helpful way to do that is to think of the concept of "Life Lesson Learned." Try this exercise:

Go twenty years into the future after your novel ends. Sit your Lead character down in a chair. If your Lead character happens to be dead, you get to perform a resurrection. Or you can talk to his ghost. Whatever, sit him down!

Now ask, like a reporter, this question: Looking back at all that happened to you, why do you think you had to go through that? What did you learn that you need to tell the rest of us?

Write down his answer.

In mythic structure, this is called the Return With the Elixir. As Christopher Vogler, author of *The Writer's Journey*, puts it:

> The Return with the Elixir is the final Reward earned on the Hero's Journey. The Hero has been resurrected,

> purified and has earned the right to be accepted back into the Ordinary World and share the Elixir of the Journey. The true Hero returns with an Elixir to share with others or heal a wounded land. The Elixir can be a great treasure or magic potion. It could be love, wisdom, or simply the experience of surviving the Special World. Even the tragic end of a Hero's Journey can yield the best Elixir of all, granting the audience greater awareness of us and our world (Citizen Kane). The Hero may show the benefit of the Elixir, using it to heal a physical or emotional wound, or accomplish tasks that had been feared in the Ordinary World. The Return signals a time when we distribute rewards and punishments, or celebrate the Journey's end with revelry or marriage.

What elixir (lesson) has your Lead character brought back to the community?

A Note on "The Tyranny of the Premise"

Maybe it's just me, but I've never been able to embrace the concept of "the premise." Some teachers absolutely insist upon it. Indeed, James N. Frey, in his book *How to Write a Damn Good Novel,* argues that authors must kneel before the "tyranny" of the premise.

Just what is a premise, anyway? Turns out it's just another way of expressing theme or meaning. It's a conflict of values leading to a moral conclusion. Lajos Egri, in *The Art of Dramatic Writing*, illustrates with examples such as:

Foolish generosity leads to poverty.

Craftiness digs its own grave.

Dissipation leads to self-destruction.

And so on. You know what that sounds like? A short version of your Lead character's life lesson. And the stuff of the elixir.

Do you need to know your meaning before you begin writing? I suppose some writers like to work from a premise, but truth be told I've not met many. It is too much like writing in order to prove something, and such fiction can come off as too manipulative or out of balance. That's probably the main thrust of my resistance to the term *premise.* Also the word *tyranny.* Who likes tyrant? Writing is hard enough.

To be fair, neither Frey nor Egri insist you have to start with a premise in mind before you write. You can find it later, during the writing or revision.

I just like *life lesson* better because it sounds more like the real-life struggle of the character in the novel.

Try this:

Take three of your favorite novels and write out the theme as a life lesson learned. Do it in the voice of the Lead character.

7

BRAINSTORMING ENDINGS

Don't skip this section, pantsers! You may be so against planning that your knickers get in a twist (even if you don't wear knickers), but what I'm telling you here will prove helpful.

Several times in my career I've decided to write a novel just by getting an idea for a great climactic scene. I've envisioned courtroom dramas, unique deaths, and sometimes emotionally resonant scenes between characters

I once wrote a whole screenplay because I pictured a father-son reconciliation scene while listening to the musical rendition of "Unchained Melody." That scene was so powerful to me that I wanted to write the script just to find out how to get there.

I did write the script, and sent it to Ed Harris, but never heard back, which is a pity because it would have earned him a Best Actor Oscar.

Ahem.

You will note, of course, that this is one step further than knowing the ending shape (as discussed in Chapter 5). This is more specific and therefore more emotional to you, the author.

Emotion is the great driving force of fiction, so the more of it you have for your story, the better.

Remember, a specific ending is not etched in stone. It's always subject to change without notice. But the added inner fire it gives you will elevate all your writing.

Further, having a specific ending in place before you start writing opens up all sorts of organic story and scene ideas. The brainstormed ending is your writer's mind sending you a message. It's saying there's something deep here and I want you to explore it!

Alfred Hitchcock's classic, *North By Northwest*, came about because Hitch envisioned a climactic chase across the giant stone heads of Mount Rushmore. He hired a well-known screenwriter, Ernest Lehman, to flesh out everything else. And boy, did he.

I've heard mystery writers say something along the following lines: *I just write. I write without knowing who committed the murder. Because if I don't know who the murderer is, it's pretty certain the reader won't, either.*

While this sentiment sounds logical, it is based on a false dichotomy. If you do know who your killer is going to be that does not, perforce, mean the reader will have a clue. The art of writing a mystery is in the hiding of things, the red herrings, and the skillful reveal. You don't get those things simply by virtue of not knowing who the villain is beforehand.

Let's just say this line of thought is more or less fodder for the pantsing writer. Which is fine as long as you realize that your first draft is for discovery, and once discovered you'll have a lot of re-writing to do.

That's one approach.

The other is to know your ending so you can plant clues and red herrings skillfully and purposefully all along the way.

This doesn't mean you have to massively outline your novel before writing it. As one of the great twisty-turny thriller writers, Harlan Coben (a non-outliner) has said, knowing the ending makes the writing "like driving from New Jersey to California. I may go Route 60, I may go via the Straits of Magellan or stop over in Tokyo . . . but I'll end up in California."

So how do you brainstorm an ending?

I like using music. As I mentioned above, it was a piece of music that gave me the ending scene for one of the great unmade screenplays in Hollywood history.

I am partial to movie soundtracks. I have them playlisted by mood—heartfelt, suspense, action, love, and so on. I use these for writing scenes and picturing characters, and especially for brainstorming endings.

As the music plays, close your eyes and let a movie unfold in your mind. Don't stop it, just watch it. Allow your characters to improvise. Let them jump into different settings. Eventually, one of them is going to hit you on an emotional level, and that's when you stop and jot down a note about the scene.

Repeat with other music.

Pretty soon, you'll have a list of possible endings. Which carries with it the deepest impact? You don't have to make sense out of it completely, not at this point. What you want is something to write toward. That's all you need.

If you are a plotter, you can create your outline with this ending in mind.

If you are a pantser, the ending will be there for you, a long way away, just to keep you from falling off a cliff.

There's another point where you should brainstorm, and that is when you are almost finished with the book.

Perhaps your original ending still works. That's a bonus. Use it!

If you're not sure, then use my SPAD method: *Stew, Brew, Accrue, Do.*

I detail this method to you out of professional obligation, because it works for me. But because I am not a doctor (nor do I play one on TV), I advise simply that you take this with a grain of coffee and modify it to fit your needs.

Stew

By the time I reach the last fifty pages of my novel, I pretty much know how it is going to end. I've had an ending in mind from the beginning and it was part of my plot map.

But as the novel progresses, other ideas surface. That can't be helped, and is in fact a good thing. It's your manuscript taking on real life and generating stuff you could not anticipate until you started writing.

So as I go into the home stretch, I've modified my ending with notes I've jotted during the writing itself.

The last signposts of my novels are: Q Factor, Final Battle, Transformation, Resonance. (The signpost method for writing a novel I cover in the book *Super Structure.*)

I begin to stew about it. That means just thinking. When I'm not at the keyboard I'm walking around visualizing the scene in my mind and just letting it be up there playing around.

When it comes time to begin writing those pages, I will do

an intense stew. I'll sit down for an hour or more and think intensely about the final scenes. I will think about all the things that need to be accomplished, like tying up loose ends, thematic images, showing the Lead's transformation. I will make notes, usually handwritten notes because that gets another part of my brain involved.

At the end of that session there are a lot of ingredients in my stew, being cooked. I want to let them simmer.

Brew

What I do then is put aside all thought on the project, plug in the earbuds and iTunes, and take a nice long walk. This walk is the opportunity for the boys in the basement to get to work while I relax.

The walk is not random. It is headed toward a local coffee house. If you are not within walking distance of such a place, drive your car near the location and take a walk around several blocks before coming back for the Brew aspect of the process.

I order a double espresso. Now I realize there are those for whom caffeine is not an agreeable part of their diet, or who think that the stimulation of the coffee bean is in some way unhelpful or unhealthful. Certainly you can overdo it, like poor old Balzac, who died of caffeine poisoning at the age of 51 because of the thick mud he used to down throughout the day and night.

But I like a little caffeinated stimulation from time to time. I believe the current wisdom is that the moderate intake of caffeine has health benefits. I'll go with that until further notice.

I sit down at a table and sip my brew for a few minutes. Then I take out a physical notebook and pen.

Accrue

Now I collect all of the thoughts, images, bits of dialogue, and whatever else has been bubbling down there in the basement. I like using paper for this, because I can doodle, do mind maps. As I jot down ideas some will connect with others and I can draw a line from a note to another note.

Let me give you an example. Here is a bit of the paper I used when I was writing the ending for my zombie legal thriller, *I Ate The Sheriff.*

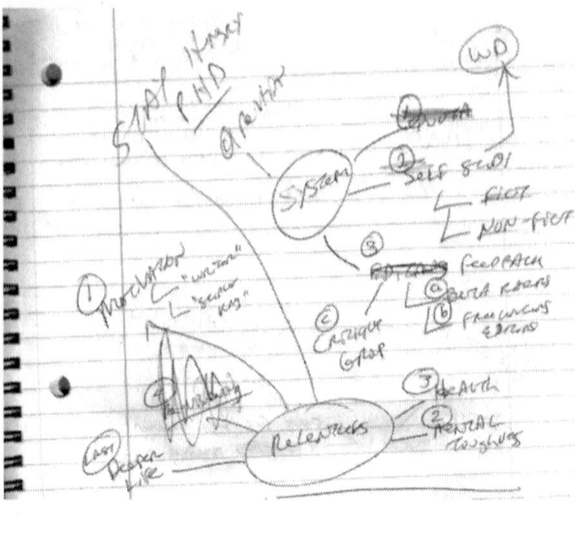

Note the numbers I added. This was at the end of the process and gave me the order of the scenes. It was my final outline for the last fifty pages.

Do

Now back at my keyboard I am ready to write, to work on those last pages with all the fervor that I can. All of the stew, all of the ideas, all of the mind maps, have come together for me. I simply do the best job I can until I reach that satisfying moment when I can place the final punctuation mark of the entire manuscript.

It may take me a day or several to get the final pages done, but I try to do them in as timely a fashion as possible.

Perhaps I should add one final stage, and call it *Woohoo.* This is the celebration moment when I finish a manuscript, and I know I won't have to think about it for at least six weeks. That's the usual amount of time I give myself to set aside a first draft before beginning the revision process. That starts with a first read-through of a hard copy, taking minimal notes.

I then give the manuscript to some beta readers. After that it's second draft time, and then a final polish.

I mention the polish because there is one final step in the crafting of an ending that I leave until the very end of the revision process.

It's the all-important element of resonance, which is the subject of our next chapter.

8

RESONANT ENDINGS

Resonance is that last, perfect note in a great piece of music, leaving the audience not just satisfied, but moved. Perhaps even changed.

Just like a novel with the perfect last lines, which can take a novel that is good and move it to unforgettable.

The Woman in the Window is the mega-bestselling thriller by A. J. Finn. The lead character is Dr. Anna Fox, who was a prominent child psychologist. Now she lives alone, suffering from a bad case of agoraphobia—the fear of going outside—due to a trauma she suffered a year earlier. In a plot reminiscent of the great Hitchcock movie, *Rear Window,* Anna sees something disturbing in a neighbor's window, and the suspense builds from there. I won't give away the plot twists here, but I do want you to have a look at the last lines. Because after everything that happens, and it's all wrapped up, we're still left wondering if Anna is ever going to get over her current condition. At the very end her friend and physical therapist, Bina, is trying to coax Anna to step outside.

> She releases my hand and walks into the garden, tracking footprints in the snow. She turns, beckons me.
>
> "Come on."
>
> I close my eyes.
>
> And open them.
>
> And step into the light.

You see here how often in a thriller the last line resonance is, most of the time, something to do with the inner life of the character. As it should be. There is a transformation here, a gaining of strength. And notice the word *light*. It's a word that carries significance, like *soul*.

In *The Godfather*, after the chapter where Michael proves his transformation into a cold-hearted mafia don who can look in his wife's eyes and lie, we have an epilogue.

It's a year later. Kay has left Michael, taking their two children, because she found out he lied to her about Carlo Rizzi's murder. The family lawyer, Tom Hagen, visits her and explains why Michael did what he did, that he had been betrayed by one of the trusted inner circle, Tessio, and that Carlo had helped to set up Sonny's assassination, and that they were both a threat to the family, to the children.

Kay takes it all in, and makes the difficult decision to return to Michael.

At the very end, she has entered a Catholic church to receive Holy Communion:

> Washed clean of sin, a favored supplicant, she bowed her head and folded her hands over the altar rail. She shifted her body to make her weight less punishing to her knees. She emptied her mind of all thought of herself, of her children, of all anger, of all rebellion, of all questions.

> Then with a profound and deeply willed desire to believe, to be heard, as she had done every day since the murder of Carlo Rizzi, she said the necessary prayers for the soul of Michael Corleone.

The resonance here is built upon the words *soul* and *prayers*. They are perfect final notes.

This is the ending of *To Kill A Mockingbird:*

> He turned out the light and went into Jem's room. He would be there all night, and he would be there when Jem waked up in the morning.

To gain resonance like this, it's helpful to think of certain forms of final scenes that have worked well over time. Here are some of the most popular forms:

"Into the Sunset"

Casablanca resonates with a walk "into the sunset" (thought it's actually into the fog at night). This is a metaphor for a type of ending where a character, after all the trouble has been resolved, "rides off" like the old Western hero, into the setting sun. It gives us a feeling of completion, which can be hopeful or bittersweet.

It can be a feeling of hope, or a feeling of sadness.

In *Casablanca,* we have hope. There's been a resurrection. Rick was a dead man walking. Then Ilsa came back and the past was hashed out, as was Rick's moral deadness. As he and Louis walk off together, the effect is going up to heaven—the foggy airport is like clouds, and the airfield lights like stars.

Bittersweet is the feeling one gets from the sunset ending

of *My Name is Asher Lev* by Chiam Potok. The setting is a Hasidic community in 1950s Brooklyn. At the end, the community—including Asher's parents—have coldly reacted to Asher's art. So much so that the local Rebbe tells Asher he can no longer live among them. He is hurting too many people.

Asher's parents are crushed, but know also that it must be so. As does Asher. He has to choose between his background and his future. The novel ends:

> I came out of the apartment house. It was cold and dark. I looked up. My parents stood framed in the living-room window. I hailed a cab and climbed inside. It pulled slowly away from the curb. I turned in the seat and looked out the rear window of the cab. My parents were still watching me through our living-room window.

What's beautiful and heartbreaking here is one word—*our.* Asher still sees that apartment as home, but he cannot live there anymore.

This is why just the right words are crucial for the resonant ending.

Potok's ending has the same feel—the uncertain future but a past that must be left behind—as Charles Webb's *The Graduate.* The ending image in the film is the same as in the book: a bus driving off "into the sunset." Inside the bus sit Benjamin Braddock and the newly married Elaine Robinson, wearing her wedding dress.

Wait, what?

Elaine has just married Carl Smith. Benjamin bursts into the church and runs up to the balcony and shouts, "Elaine!"

Elaine responds by running out of the church with Ben.

They get to a bus that is just pulling away. Ben pounds on the door. The driver lets them in. They go to the back of the bus as everyone, including the driver, stares at them.

> "Get it moving!" Benjamin said, beginning to rise up again from the seat. "Get this bus moving!"
>
> The driver waited a moment, then turned around and climbed back into his seat. He pulled a handle and the doors of the bus closed. Benjamin sat back down.
>
> Elaine was still trying to catch her breath. She turned her face to look at him. For several moments she sat looking at him, then she reached over and took his hand.
>
> "Benjamin?" she said.
>
> "What."
>
> The bus began to move.

That is the perfect ending for this bittersweet novel. The lovers are off "into the sunset," but without any certainty about what the future holds.

Completing the Circle

This is applicable to the *frame story*. A frame story is a novel that begins in the present, with a narrator recounting the story that happened in the past. It finishes with a final scene or moment in the present, giving the impression that we've come full circle.

Stephen King's *The Green Mile* is such a novel. It begins in the present, in a nursing home, where the narrator, Paul Edgecombe reflects back to 1932, when he was working as the supervising guard on Death Row of a penitentiary. It is the story of some of the condemned men, but most specifically John Coffey, a huge black man convicted of killing two white girls. After the extraordinary events, the book returns to the present, to a final scene with the elderly Edgecombe.

A satisfying ending to a frame story can come via straight narration, as in *The Green Mile*:

> I look back over these pages, leafing through them with my trembling, spotted hands, and I wonder if there is some meaning here, as in those books which are supposed to be uplifting and ennobling… Sometimes I doze and see that underpass in the rain, with John Coffey standing beneath it in the shadows. It's never just a trick of the eye, in these little dreams; it's always him for sure, my big boy, just standing there and watching. I lie here and wait. I think about Janice, how I lost her, how she ran away red through my fingers in the rain, and I wait. We each owe a death, there are no exceptions, I know that, but sometimes, oh God, the Green Mile is so long.

A frame story can also end with a resonant line of dialogue. In his novel *The Princess Bride,* William Goldman uses a framing device—a fictionalized account of his life in the present day and his history with the S. Morgenstern tale of "true love and high adventure." A more illustrative frame story is in Goldman's movie script. It begins with a grandfather (Peter Falk) summoned to read to his ailing grandson (Fred Savage). The boy is not excited about this prospect, but promises to try to stay awake.

"Thank you very much," the grandfather says. "Your vote of confidence is overwhelming."

And so he begins to read, and the story unfolds before us. Every now and then it's interrupted by the boy and we get a short scene in the present. Then back to the story of Princess Buttercup and Westley and Fezzik and Inigo.

In the story, of course, Westley the farm boy only answers "As you wish" to Buttercup when they initially meet.

The story ends with the famous kiss. As the grandfather explains, "Since the invention of the kiss, there have been five kisses that were rated the most passionate, the most pure. This one left them all behind. The end."

We are back to the opening scene now, for the closing of the frame. The grandfather tells the boy it's time to sleep, and is about to leave the room when the boy calls out to him. "Grandpa, maybe you could come over and read it again to me tomorrow."

With a twinkle in his eye, Grandpa replies, "As you wish."

Perfect—using a dialogue line from the story to gently close the frame.

The Ah and the Uh-Oh!

Another way to think of a resonant ending is by way of the *Ah* or the *Uh-oh!* These describe the feeling that a reader is left with. The story satisfies in a happy fashion, or leaves open the distinct possibility that something just as bad, or worse, may soon take place!

The Ah

The *Ah* ending is a combination of both the last scene and the perfect last line (as in *Casablanca.*)

At the end of Michael Connelly's *Lost Light* (my favorite of the Harry Bosch series), Bosch discovers that he has a daughter. She is presented to him by the mother, Eleanor, Bosch's ex-wife. It's obviously a stunning revelation. Which leads to this paragraph:

> Twin skyrockets were going off inside me. One left a trail of red, the other green. They were going different ways. One anger, one warmth. One led to the heart's dark abyss, a devil's punchbowl filled with recriminations and revenge I could dip my cup fully into. The other led away from all of that. To Paradise Road. To bright, blessed days and dark, sacred nights. It led to the place where lost light came from. My lost light.

Conflicting emotions are always a good move in fiction. They create emotional cross-currents in the reader, and tell us that the moment is about high personal stakes.

There couldn't be any higher than this for Harry Bosch.

> I knew I could choose one path but not both. I looked up from the girl to Eleanor. She had tears on her face and yet a smile. I knew then what path to choose and that there is no end to things of the heart. I stepped forward and squatted down in front of the girl. I knew from dealing with young witnesses that it was best to approach them on their level.
>
> "Hello, Maddie," I said to my daughter.
>
> She turned her face and pushed it into her mother's leg.
>
> "I'm too shy," she said.
>
> "That's okay, Maddie. I'm pretty shy myself. Can I just hold your hand?"
>
> She let go of her mother's hand and extended hers to me. I took it and she wrapped her tiny fingers around my

> index finger. I shifted forward until my knees were on the floor and I was sitting back on my heels. She peeked her eyes out at me. She didn't seem scared. Just cautious. I raised my other hand and she gave me her other hand, the fingers wrapping the same way around my one.
>
> I leaned forward and raised her tiny fists and held them against my closed eyes. In that moment I knew all the mysteries were solved. That I was home. That I was saved.

This is a prime example of the personal ending in a thriller or crime novel. When the main action is over, a subplot dealing with the Lead's personal life is brought to a resolution.

When done well, as Connelly does so often, the feeling created is supremely satisfying. It's as if the author is saying no matter how bad, dark, evil the world is, there is the possibility of safety, of closure, of peace.

The Uh-Oh!

With the *Uh-oh*, the feeling is left that there is more trouble to come. Maybe a lot more. And we get to fill in the blanks ourselves.

In Louis L'Amour's bestseller *Last of the Breed*, Joe Mack, a half-Sioux-American Air Force pilot, is captured by Soviets during the Cold War and imprisoned in Siberia. It's the task of Soviet Col. Arkady Zamatev to squeeze information out of Mack.

But he escapes the prison, which is deemed a stupid thing to do, for the winter is coming in Siberia. How can Mack expect to survive?

Because he is the last of the warrior breed, and his Indian skills come into play for survival.

Zamatev dispatches the Russian analogue of Mack—a Yakut named Alekhin—to do the tracking. The heart of the book is their back and forth, the narrow escapes, the body count.

Finally, at the end of the book, Alekhin and Mack are face to face. It's time for the fight to the finish.

At this point L'Amour cuts to the last scene, in Col. Zamatev's point of view. He has received a package—something wrapped up in cloth.

It is a scalp.

There is a note inside also, written on birchbark. It says:

> *This was once a custom of my people. In my lifetime I shall take two. This is the first.*

Uh-oh!

A genre which is a natural for the *Uh-oh* ending is horror. And who better to illustrate its use than Mr. Stephen King? At the end of *Pet Sematary,* summarized earlier in this book, Louis Creed is alone, playing solitaire, when the back door opens. Louis doesn't even turn around. "Slow, gritting footsteps" approach. The steps end behind him.

> A cold hand fell on Louis's shoulder. Rachel's voice was grating, full of dirt.
>
> "Darling," it said.

Yes, Louis Creed got his wife back.

But . . . uh oh!

The Twist in the Tail

In *Writing a Thriller,* André Jute describes the twist in the tail as a "secondary, unexpected climax which often turns everything the reader has been led to believe on its head."

> When I started writing, I used to regard these "kickers" in the novels of published writers with great envy, but now I know it is an easier technique than, for instance, the properly placed and controlled flashback. You merely take your second most favorite ending for the story and then go back and plant a few clues to the twist in the tail so that the reader is not cheated, not forgetting at the same time to water down any overly explicit clues because making it too easy for the reader is another no-no.

Jute gives us the technique right there. When you are brainstorming the actual content of your ending (did you catch *Brew, Stew, Accrue, Do, Woohoo* earlier in this book?) come up with a second, third, and perhaps even fourth possibility. If one of them seems the best, use it. But then use, as Jute advises, the next-best as the twist.

Foreshadowing

Your resonant ending can be rendered all the more powerful by *foreshadowing.* A good definition of the term comes from the site LiteraryDevices.net:

> Foreshadowing is a literary device in which a writer gives an advance hint of what is to come later in the story. Foreshadowing often appears at the beginning of a story,

> or a chapter, and helps the reader develop expectations about the coming events in a story. There are various ways to create foreshadowing.
>
> A writer may use character dialogues to hint at what may occur in the future. In addition, any event or action in the story may throw a hint to the readers about future events or actions.

When such a hint is finally paid off, the emotional impact is richly satisfying.

Which is why I developed a technique I call *the argument against transformation.* It is one of my 14 structural signposts. Briefly stated, have your Lead character express, sometime in Act 1, an idea about himself or life that is the opposite of how things turn out at the end.

In *Casablanca,* Rick argues that he sticks his neck out for nobody. At the end, he sticks it out for Ilsa and Victor.

In *It's a Wonderful Life,* what is the life lesson learned at the end? It's that no man is a failure if he stays in his own home town and lives a life helping his neighbors. But that's not what the young George Bailey thinks.

In the flashback sequence about his boyhood, we find George working in the drug store. Mary and Violet are there and George tells them he's going to be an explorer someday, and pointedly says he's going to have a harem, and maybe three or four wives.

The resonance of the ending is enhanced by this, for he will have but one wife, whom he loves deeply; and one hometown, which loves him deeply.

So, if the character transforms into a better version of himself at the end, have him express the opposite view in the beginning. In *On the Waterfront,* the classic American film starring Marlon Brando and Eva Marie Saint, Brando plays Terry Malloy, a waterfront thug for the local mob. But then he starts falling for the sister of a guy who was killed by the mob, with Malloy's unwitting assistance.

The thrust of the movie is whether Terry Malloy will have the courage to expose the mob to the waterfront crime commission, effectively putting his life in jeopardy. Through the love of Edie (played by Saint) and the murder of his brother Charley (Rod Steiger), he does take that step.

But in Act 1, while sharing a beer with Edie, he argues the exact opposite. Edie says you have to care about other people, and Terry calls her a fruitcake. Then he says the only thing to do is whatever it takes to keep alive, and mix with the "right" people, so you have "a little change jangling in your pocket."

Edie says that's living like an animal. And Terry shrugs and says, "I'd rather live like an animal than end up like. . ."

He suddenly realizes he's about to name her dead brother, and stops. She finishes for him. "Like Joey? Are you afraid to mention his name?"

By the end of the film, Terry has learned how bad the bad guys are, and that humanity demands he stand up to them.

It's all the more powerful because we know how far Terry has come.

Two other forms of foreshadowing to consider:

Dialogue

A line of dialogue from the opening pages can come back for a power punch as the last line of the book. One of the most stunning noir novels ever written is *Nightmare Alley* by

William Lindsay Gresham, published in 1946. It's the story of Stan Carlisle, a hustler working as a magician in a carnival. The carnival features the grotesque attraction known as "the geek," a sub-human who bites the heads off live chickens.

In the first chapter, Stan asks the head of the carny where on earth he finds such a character. The head guy levels with Stan—you don't find them, you make them. You find a drunk, a real boozer down on his luck, and...

> "... you tell him like this: 'I got a little job for you. It's a temporary job. We got to get a new geek. So until we do you'll put on the geek outfit and fake it.'"

In other words, just use a hidden razor to nick the chicken's neck and pretend to drink the blood. (Yes, there really were such "attractions" back in the day.)

The man continues:

> "Well, he does this for a week and you see to it he gets his bottle regular and a place to sleep it off in. He likes this fine. This is what he thinks is heaven. So after a week you say to him like this, you say, 'Well, I got to get me a real geek. You're through.' He scares up at this because nothing scares a real rummy like the chance of a dry spell and getting the horrors ... You give him time to think it over, while you're talking. Then throw in the chicken. He'll geek."

The rest of the novel is about the rise and fall of Stan Carlisle. He begins a spiritualist act as a way to bilk the bereaved out of their money. The cost to his psyche is too great. By the end of the book Stan is a drunk on the lam.

One night he stumbles, bombed and filthy, into the office of another carnival manager. He offers to become a palm reading act, but the manager doesn't need one. Instead, recognizing an opportunity, he gives Stan a couple of belts of booze. The final lines of the book:

> The lush was already back in the chair, leaning forward, his hands spread against his chest, elbows on the chair arms, head lolling. "Hey mister, how 'bout 'nother li'l shot 'fore I go?"
>
> "Yeah, sure. But I just happened to think of something. I got one job you might take a crack at. It ain't much, and I ain't begging you to take it, but it's a job. Keep you in coffee and cakes and a shot now and then. What do you say? Of course, it's only temporary—just until we get a real geek."

Wow. And uh-oh.

Images

Visual motifs are powerful in fiction, especially so when used as foreshadowing. My novel *Glimpses of Paradise* is a historical following two Midwestern high school kids from just before World War I through early 1920s Hollywood.

Zee Miller is a spirited girl from the wrong side of the tracks. Doyle Lawrence is the son of a prominent citizen. According to Doyle's family, Zee is not the right girl for him. But he can't help but be drawn to her.

In the first chapter Zee and Doyle are in the town park, arguing. Suddenly Zee takes off her shoes and climbs a tree.

Doyle yells at her to get down. She calls him a wet blanket. He threatens to climb up after her, hoping she'll relent.

> Instead, she giggled, and he saw her reach her arm up toward the sky. It was a gesture of such verve and confidence it froze Doyle in place. The audacity of it! She had no fear of falling, no fear of anything it seemed. Least of all his pursuit.
>
> Electricity rushed through Doyle and he began to climb.
>
> Still laughing, Zee pulled herself up to the higher limbs.

At the end of the book, Zee sacrifices her life to save Doyle from mobsters. The final chapter takes place four years later. Doyle is back in the same park, with his family, his wife, Molly, and young daughter, Isabel. All's well, and then Doyle's sister, Gertie, runs over:

> She was shaking her head and pointing. "Doyle, come."
>
> "What is it?"
>
> "That daughter of yours. She's up a tree!"
>
> Doyle got to his feet and looked where Gertie pointed. Indeed, Isabel was halfway up a tree. Doyle's mind surged with remembrance. It was the same tree Zee Miller had once climbed, years ago when they were together in the park. The tree he'd fallen out of right under her nose.
>
> "What are you going to do?" Gertie asked.
>
> "Nothing."
>
> "Nothing? But what if she falls?"
>
> "She's not going to fall."

Isabel's voice sang down from the tree. "Papa! Mama! Look!"

Molly rushed to Doyle's side. "Do you think she'll be all right?"

Doyle put his arm around his wife. "I know she will."

"Look!" Isabel Lawrence chirped, and reached toward the sky.

Try this:

- Once you have your ending in place, find a moment in an early scene in Act 1 where the character espouses the opposite of what she believes at the end. The best way to do that is through a dialogue exchange with another character.
- Work and re-work your last 250 words, especially the last few sentences. Go not just for the right ending, but the right *sound.* Break up the last 100 words of your novel into lines of four or five words, creating a poem. Edit the poem then put the lines back together.
- Consider an image or line of dialogue to end your novel. Use an image/line from the opening pages, or create it at the end and go back and plant it in the opening.

9

AVOIDING COMMON ENDING PROBLEMS

Here are the most common ending mistakes. Avoid them so your readers don't get to the end and throw the book (or their Kindle) across the room!

Deus Ex Machina

From the Latin, *deus ex machina* literally means "god from the machine." As the Encyclopedia Britannica explains:

> The term was first used in ancient Greek and Roman drama, where it meant the timely appearance of a god to unravel and resolve the plot. The *deus ex machina* was named for the convention of the god's appearing in the sky, an effect achieved by means of a crane (Greek: *mēchanē*). The dramatic device dates from the 5th century BC; a god appears in Sophocles' *Philoctetes* and in most of the plays of Euripides to solve a crisis by divine intervention.
>
> Since ancient times, the phrase has also been applied to an unexpected savior or to an improbable event that brings

order out of chaos (e.g., the arrival, in time to avert tragedy, of the U.S. cavalry in a western film).

The reason this is a mistake is that the reader expects the Lead to overcome (or die trying) by strength of will. Having the unexpected and unjustified intervention of another party violates this implied guarantee.

The unexpected can be another character just showing up—or a coincidence that happens—at just the right time.

Which is not to say that another character or force cannot show up in time to rescue the Lead from a terrible situation. It does mean, however, *that the Lead must have set in place the circumstances and rationale for this intervention earlier in the book.*

When Richard Kimble in the movie *The Fugitive* is being targeted by the Chicago police, who will shoot him on sight, it is the Deputy U.S. Marshal, Sam Gerard, who gets to him first and saves him. But the reason he does is that Kimble, throughout the last half of the story, has shown Gerard through his actions that he had been railroaded by the Chicago police. Gerard, despite his philosophy of "I don't care," can't help himself. He finds the Chicago cops to be less than forthcoming.

So it was Kimble's own strength of will, his fighting back, and his inexplicable return to Chicago (the scene of the murder) that creates the circumstances for Gerard to show up and save him at the end.

The lesson is simple: No coincidence can get your Lead out of the final battle. Nor can another character, unless the Lead has put the right circumstances into place.

Loose Ends

It's not uncommon for a writer of mysteries or thrillers—especially if said writer is of the pantser species—to get to the end of a manuscript with some dangling loose ends. For example, let's say you've written a mystery with lots of clues and red herrings. At the end of the book the detective or sleuth reveals the answers, except for something that happened to a character earlier in the book. He doesn't have the means to know that information.

What do you do? The solution is quite simple. In her book, *Dynamic Characters*, Nancy Kress counsels that for loose ends you work backward, through your *secondary characters.* You can have a minor character from another part of the book make an appearance and deliver the information. He could say, "Did you hear that the accountant who was hiding the books jumped off a building?"

Or you can work the other way. Just create a brand-new minor character in the climactic scene, *then* go back in the plot and plant that character in a scene or two just so that he can come in and clean up the plot thread at the end.

You know who did this all the time? Charles Dickens.

Think about *David Copperfield.* All those characters. One narrator. How to keep track of what happened to everyone?

When we get to the last fifty pages, there are two characters in particular we want to know the fate of: Little Emily and Wilkins Micawber.

So Dickens gives us the penultimate chapter where David and his wife, Agnes, get a surprise visit from Emily's father, Mr. Peggotty.

"And now tell us," says David, "everything relating to your fortunes."

Talk about giving a minor character license to wrap things up!

Mr. Peggotty gives a brief account of his current conditions. "What with sheep-farming, and what with stock-farming, and what with one thing and what with t'other, we are as well to do, as well could be."

And then David asks, "And Emily?"

Mr. Peggotty gives the bitter-sweet tale.

David asks about two other characters—Martha and Mrs. Gummidge.

Mr. Peggotty delivers the news.

Finally, David asks about Mr. Micawber. Wise novelist that he is, Dickens doesn't give us another verbal response from Mr. Peggotty. Instead, Mr. Peggotty hands David a newspaper from his little town, where Mr. Micawber happened to have settled. David reads a notice aloud, which includes the following:

> The public dinner to our distinguished fellow-colonist and townsman, WILKINS MICAWBER, ESQUIRE, Port Middlebay District Magistrate, came off yesterday in the large room of the Hotel, which was crowded to suffocation. It is estimated that not fewer than forty-seven persons must have been accommodated with dinner at one time, exclusive of the company in the passage and on the stairs…Doctor Mell, in a speech replete with feeling, then proposed "Our distinguished Guest, the ornament of our town. May he never leave us but to better himself, and may his success among us be such as to render his bettering himself impossible!"

And because Mr. Micawber was so great a part of David's life, and vice versa, there is more. Mr. Peggotty points to another part of the paper, where Mr. Micawber placed a personal letter to "David Copperfield, Esquire, the Eminent Author." It ends, "Go on, my dear Sir, in your Eagle course! The inhabitants of Port Middlebay may at least aspire to watch it, with delight, with entertainment, with instruction!" It is signed *Wilkins Micawber, Magistrate.*

But that's not all. Dickens (wise novelist again!) gives us a resonant ending to the chapter:

> We talked much of Mr. Micawber, on many other evenings while Mr. Peggotty remained with us. He lived with us during the whole term of his stay,—which, I think, was something less than a month,—and his sister and my aunt came to London to see him. Agnes and I parted from him aboard-ship, when he sailed; and we shall never part from him more, on earth.
>
> But before he left, he went with me to Yarmouth, to see a little tablet I had put up in the churchyard to the memory of Ham. While I was copying the plain inscription for him at his request, I saw him stoop, and gather a tuft of grass from the grave and a little earth.
>
> 'For Em'ly,' he said, as he put it in his breast. 'I promised, Mas'r Davy.'

Only a Dream

Perhaps the greatest mistake of all, and the biggest letdown, is the *It was all a dream* ending. It's so bad that it doesn't seem to happen much anymore. But there are variations.

Instead of a dream, the reason could be a vision before death, as in the movie *Jacob's Ladder.* (I recall a local movie critic who thought most of the movie was gripping, "Until the ending, which, frankly, stinks.")

Or the "dream" could be the result of some high-tech operation on the brain. But if it's left to be revealed at the end, with no way for the reader to figure it out beforehand, the result is the same—massive disappointment. This happened with a novel by a master of Twilight Zone-esque plots, Richard Matheson (who wrote some of the best Zones, and many famous stories that were turned into movies or TV episodes). His novel *7 Steps to Midnight* is a page-turner of the *how can this possibly be happening?* variety. But then, as Kirkus put it in their review, "all this nearly arbitrary mayhem [is] explained away in an absurdly far-fetched premise."

Interestingly, these types of endings can work in shorter forms of fiction. The "vision before death" story was made famous by Ambrose Bierce in "An Occurrence at Owl Creek Bridge." And many a Twilight Zone had a story-altering twist ending, such as Matheson's own script "A World of Difference," which has a plot that resembles *7 Steps to Midnight.* The ending works in the shorter version because it was consistent with the design of the show.

But a novel doesn't come with that same design. It's expected to make sense at the end, or at least offer a solution that doesn't come from so far out in left field that it's actually in the parking lot.

The Talkative Villain

How many times have we seen this in movies, TV shows, and thrillers: The villain finally has the good guy at his mercy. Death is inevitable. Yet the bad guy doesn't pull the trigger.

Or push the hero off the building. Or drop him into a pool of piranha.

Instead, the villain decides to *explain everything* to the hero.

Which gives the hero time to get a piece of broken glass with which to saw the rope his wrists are bound in.

Or allows the hero's ally to arrive to save him.

Rule of thumb: don't put the villain's big explanation just before the means of rescue or escape. Instead, drop it in earlier when the urgency to kill the good guy is not so great. Or wait until *after* the villain is dispatched and give the explanation to another character. (Perhaps the most famous example of the latter is the speech given by the psychiatrist at the end of Alfred Hitchcock's *Psycho*.)

Not doing the wrong thing is almost as important as doing the right thing. If you avoid these mistakes your novel's resonant ending will not get lost in fog of error.

10

SOME ENDINGS EXAMINED

The Maltese Falcon

Dashiell Hammett's classic detective story, *The Maltese Falcon,* is about San Francisco private eye Sam Spade and a trio of thieves intent on getting their hands on a priceless statuette. At the beginning of the book Spade's partner, Miles Archer, is murdered. A woman named Brigid O'Shaughnessy had hired the firm to follow a man named Thursby, who is also murdered. Soon a mysterious little man named Joel Cairo shows up, looking for a "black bird." He is partners with the "fat man," Casper Gutman. Things happen (that's how you summarize a mystery plot). Eventually Spade ends up with the bird and puts it in storage. Spade then enters his apartment with Brigid, only to find Gutman, Cairo and Gutman's young gunsel, Wilmer Cook, waiting for him. Gutman wants the black bird. Negotiations begin.

The first order of business, for Spade, is electing a "fall-guy" for the three murders (Archer, Thursby, and a ship's captain named Jacobi).

The fat man frowned without comprehension, but before he could speak Spade was explaining: "The police have got to have a victim—somebody they can stick for those three murders. We—"

Cairo, speaking in a brittle excited voice, interrupted Spade. "Two—only two—murders, Mr. Spade. Thursby undoubtedly killed your partner."

"All right, two," Spade growled. "What difference does it make? The point is we've got to feed the police some—"

Now Gutman broke in, smiling confidently, talking with good-natured assurance: "Well sir, from what we've seen and heard of you I don't think we'll have to bother ourselves about that. We can leave the handling of the police to you, all right. You won't need any of our inexpert help."

"If that's what you think," Spade said, "you haven't seen or heard enough."

After arguing about this for a couple of pages, Spade suggests to Gutman that they give the cops Wilmer, the young gunsel. This naturally does not sit well with Wilmer. He wants to shoot Spade right there, but Spade reminds everyone that if he dies, no one gets the falcon.

Gutman orders Wilmer to calm down.

Spade continues his plan to turn these thieves against each other. He suggests the fall guy be Joel Cairo.

Cairo cried in a voice shrill with indignation: "Suppose we give them you, Mr. Spade, or Miss O'Shaughnessy? How about that if you're so set on giving them somebody?"

Spade smiled at the Levantine and answered him evenly. "You people want the falcon. I've got it. A fall-guy

> is part of the price I'm asking. As for Miss O'Shaughnessy"—his dispassionate glance moved to her white perplexed face and then back to Cairo and his shoulders rose and fell a fraction of an inch—"if you think she can be rigged for the part I'm perfectly willing to discuss it with you."

Eventually, Wilmer snaps and draws his gun, but Spade knocks him out. He then gives Gutman an ultimatum. Make Wilmer the fall-guy, or no bird. Gutman thinks it over, and says, "You can have him." A deal is struck with money involved:

> "That will be excellent," Gutman purred. "Then, sir, in exchange for the ten thousand dollars and Wilmer you will give us the falcon and an hour or two of grace—so we won't be in the city when you surrender him to the authorities."
>
> "You don't have to duck," Spade said. "It'll be air-tight."

Spade calls his secretary, Effie Perine, and tells her where to find the package and to bring it by. She does.

And now the moment they've all been waiting for:

> Gutman's fat fingers made short work of cord and paper and excelsior, and he had the black bird in his hands. "Ah," he said huskily, "now, after seventeen years!" His eyes were moist.
>
> Cario licked his red lips and worked his hands together. The girl's lower lip was between her teeth. She and Cairo, like Gutman, and like Spade and the boy, were breathing

heavily. The air in the room was chilly and stale, and thick with tobacco smoke.

Gutman set the bird down on the table again and fumbled at a pocket. "It's it," he said, "but we'll make sure." Sweat glistened on his round cheeks. His fingers twitched as he took out a gold pocket-knife and opened it.

Cairo and the girl stood close to him, one on either side. Spade stood back a little where he could watch the boy as well as the group at the table.

Gutman turned the bird upside-down and scraped an edge of its base with his knife. Black enamel came off in tiny curls, exposing blackened metal beneath. Gutman's knife-blade bit into the metal, turning back a thick curved shaving. The inside of the shaving, and the narrow plane its removal had left, had the soft grey sheen of lead.

Gutman's breath hissed between his teeth. His face became turgid with hot blood. He twisted the bird around and hacked at its head. There too the edge of his knife bared lead. He let knife and bird bang down on the table while he wheeled to confront Spade. "It's a fake," he said hoarsely.

After this stunning discovery, a lot of noise is made among the thieves, until Gutman announces his desire to continue the search, by way of Constantinople. Joel Cairo agrees to go with him.

That leaves Sam Spade with Brigid O'Shaughnessy, for whom he is attracted (like a fly to a spider). She, however, killed his partner, Miles Archer, and someone has to "take the fall."

Like her! He tries to explain:

> "When a man's partner is killed he's supposed to do something about it. It doesn't make any difference what you thought of him. He was your partner and you're supposed to do something about it. Then it happens we were in the detective business. Well, when one of your organization gets killed it's bad business to let the killer get away with it. It's bad all around—bad for that one organization, bad for every detective everywhere."

So Spade turns her in to the police.

The movie ends with a line that is not in the book, but is the perfect resonance. When Detective Polhaus (played by Ward Bond) asks about the bird, "What is it?" Spade says, "The stuff that dreams are made of."

(Bonus trivia question you can use on your friends. Ask them what the last line of the movie is. Most will say *The stuff that dreams are made of*, but they'd be wrong. Ward Bond says, "Huh?")

So here we have a twist: it's not the real bird! And another: Spade is going to turn the woman he loves over to the cops for the noose, or at least a long stretch in the joint. And all the loose ends are wrapped up.

By the way, the novel ends with Spade back in his office, with Effie, ready for another day.

But this is a Lead Loses ending. Spade has lost his chance at a nice payoff, and also the woman he loves. While he has managed to solve the murder of Miles Archer, that was a subplot goal. He has at least proven his worth as a professional. As he remarks to Effie, "Your Sam's a detective."

Try this:

Give your Lead character a speech at the very end. *You don't have to use it in the book.* The primary reason is to have your Lead explain himself, justify his actions, and give closure to the story. If it reveals something surprising to you, find a way, in revision, to weave that theme into your text.

Huckleberry Finn

HEMINGWAY FAMOUSLY DECLARED THAT ALL OF MODERN American literature comes from one book, Mark Twain's *Huckleberry Finn.* The novel, however, was controversial from the jump. In 1885 the Concord Public Library banned it from their shelves for being "the veriest trash, suitable only for the slums."

Ahem.

Let's focus on Twain's use of the Mirror Moment, the transformation of Huck, and the resonant ending.

In the middle of the novel Huck has the opportunity to turn the runaway slave, Jim, over to some slave trackers, and receive a reward. In the culture Huck is part of this is the "right" thing to do. A slave is someone else's "property." Thus, helping Jim escape is stealing. And since stealing is agin' the Good Book, Huck is in danger of hellfire. So he's been taught.

But something makes Huck hesitate. He tells the trackers that he and the fellow on the raft (Jim in hiding) have small pox. The trackers make a quick exit.

All this causes Huck to reflect:

> They went off and I got aboard the raft, feeling bad and

> low, because I knowed very well I had done wrong, and I see it warn't no use for me to try to learn to do right; a body that don't get started right when he's little ain't got no show—when the pinch comes there ain't nothing to back him up and keep him to his work, and so he gets beat. Then I thought a minute, and says to myself, hold on; s'pose you'd a done right and give Jim up, would you felt better than what you do now? No, says I, I'd feel bad—I'd feel just the same way I do now. Well, then, says I, what's the use you learning to do right when it's troublesome to do right and ain't no trouble to do wrong, and the wages is just the same? I was stuck. I couldn't answer that. So I reckoned I wouldn't bother no more about it, but after this always do whichever come handiest at the time.

So here is Huck asking himself who he is, who he is supposed to be, and deciding for the moment that the best thing is to just not think about it. But he's teetering toward a transformation of some kind. He doesn't have the capacity (yet) to completely understand what's happening inside him. But we know whatever it is it's at the heart level.

Here is Huck's transformation late in Act 3. His inner struggle is too much to bear. He wants to feel cleansed, once and for all, so he won't go to hell. He writes a note to Miss Watson—Jim's "owner"—and says he's got her slave and to send the reward money. He feels good for a moment because he's not going to go to hell now. But then he starts thinking about all that he and Jim had been through:

> I'd see him standing my watch on top of his'n, 'stead of calling me, so I could go on sleeping; and see him how glad he was when I come back out of the fog; and when

> I come to him again in the swamp, up there where the feud was; and such-like times; and would always call me honey, and pet me and do everything he could think of for me, and how good he always was; and at last I struck the time I saved him by telling the men we had small-pox aboard, and he was so grateful, and said I was the best friend old Jim ever had in the world, and the only one he's got now; and then I happened to look around and see that paper.

Huck takes up the letter and suddenly freezes,

> because I'd got to decide, forever, betwixt two things, and I knowed it. I studied a minute, sort of holding my breath, and then says to myself: 'All right, then, I'll go to hell'—and tore it up.

One of the most powerful transformations in all of literature. Indeed, the esteemed Prof. Arnold Weinstein of Brown University calls it "[a]rguably the greatest moment in American fiction." By ripping up the letter Huck proves his transformation, his breaking free from a false moral prison into nascent humanity. It finds completion in the famous last lines:

> But I reckon I got to light out for the Territory ahead of the rest, because Aunt Sally she's going to adopt me and sivilize me, and I can't stand it. I been there before.

That's how you make a classic. A moral dilemma, a Mirror Moment, a crisis of conscience, a final decision, proof of transformation, and a resonant last line.

This is a "Lead Sacrifices" ending. Huck has sacrificed his

soul (in his own mind) for a greater moral good. The reward he gets is his freedom—from the "sivilization" of his culture.

Try this:

Create a real moral dilemma for your Lead character. A true dilemma is a choice between two paths, both of which carry a major cost. The decision that is made can form the heart of your story, as well as the resonance at the end.

The Hunger Games

SUZANNE COLLINS' THRILLER IS THE STORY OF 16-YEAR-OLD Katniss Everdeen and her fight to survive the deadly game of hunting and killing put on by the Capitol in the land of Panem. Katniss is a classic anti-hero, wanting only to take care of her family through illegal hunting and other such schemes. But then she becomes a default hero and rebellion leader through the course of the trilogy.

The signpost scenes are all there, such as the obvious Care Package (in which the character has a caring relationship in place; here it is Katniss' mother and sister and even a scruffy cat), and a literal Doorway of No Return:

> The moment the anthem ends, we are taken into custody. I don't mean we're handcuffed or anything, but a group of Peacekeepers marches us through the front door of the Justice Building. Maybe tributes have tried to escape in the past. I've never seen that happen though.

Once the games are underway, there's a Pet the Dog segment where Katniss helps the littlest tribute, Rue.

And then there's the romantic subplot involving Peeta Mellark. He's the boy who was kind to her once, giving her bread. Now they are supposed to kill each other. Instead, they form an alliance.

When we get to the last fifty pages, Peeta has been wounded and is slowly recovering. There is only one other tribute left, the skilled and deadly Cato.

In Chapter 24, Katniss and Peeta have some time to reflect and plan.

> When the food's cooked, I pack most of it up, leaving us each a rabbit's leg to eat as we walk. I want to move higher into the woods, climb a good tree, and make camp for the night, but Peeta resists. "I can't climb like you, Katniss, especially with my leg, and I don't think I could ever fall asleep fifty feet above the ground."
>
> "It's not safe to stay in the open, Peeta," I say.
>
> "Can't we go back to the cave?" he asks. "It's near water and easy to defend."
>
> I sigh. Several more hours of walking—or should I say crashing—through the woods to reach an area we'll just have to leave in the morning to hunt. But Peeta doesn't ask for much.

Their peace is shattered at the end of the chapter when Cato comes running at them!

> We're on our feet, Peeta wielding his knife, me poised to shoot, when Cato smashes through the trees and bears down on us. He has no spear. In fact, his hands are empty,

> yet he runs straight for us. My first arrow hits his chest and inexplicably falls aside.
>
> "He's got some kind of body armor!" I shout to Peeta.
>
> Just in time, too, because Cato is upon us. I brace myself, but he rockets right between us with no attempt to check his speed. I can tell from his panting, the sweat pouring off his purplish face, that he's been running hard a long time. Not toward us. From something. But what?

What indeed? We find out at the start of the next chapter: Muttations! Those horrific beasts created from the genetic material of the dead tributes. To paraphrase Warren Zevon, "They'll rip your lungs out, Jim."

This is the Lights Out beat signpost scene. The worst of the worse. The muttations force Cato, Peeta, and Katniss to jump on the Cornucopia for safety—and also force the Final Battle between Cato and the Katniss/Peeta team. Cato gets Peeta in a headlock, but Katniss shoots an arrow into Cato's hand. Cato falls to the muttations but is wearing body armor supplied by the Capitol. His end is long and terrible. Katniss shoots him dead "out of pity."

Now a Twist in the Tail. The Games are not over! A rule change had allowed two victors. Now it has been revoked! Only one victor will be allowed.

Bringing us to a moral dilemma.

> "Then you shoot me," I say furiously, shoving the weapons back at him. "You shoot me and go home and live with it!" And as I say it, I know death right here, right now would be the easier of the two.
>
> "You know I can't," Peeta says, discarding the weapons. "Fine, I'll go first anyway." He leans down and rips the

> bandage off his leg, eliminating the final barrier between his blood and the earth.
>
> "No, you can't kill yourself," I say. I'm on my knees, desperately plastering the bandage back onto his wound.
>
> "Katniss," he says. "It's what I want."
>
> "You're not leaving me here alone," I say. Because if he dies, I'll never go home, not really. I'll spend the rest of my life in this arena trying to think my way out.

Then Katniss figures a way out. Knowing the Capitol needs a victor, she and Peeta will threaten to eat the poison berries, right there on TV. Her plan works. Claudius Templesmith tells them to stop, and announces they have a joint victory.

Being the first book of a trilogy, Suzanne Collins leaves us with an Open-Ended Ending. We don't know what Katniss' fate is going to be vis-a-vis the Capitol. But even more, what will become of her relationship with Peeta, who now thinks that what Katniss did with him in the Games was only for show (worked out with Haymitch)? Further, what of Gale and Katniss (setting up a classic love triangle)?

> I want to tell him that he's not being fair. That we were strangers. That I did what it took to stay alive, to keep us both alive in the arena. That I can't explain how things are with Gale because I don't know myself. That it's no good loving me because I'm never going to get married anyway and he'd just end up hating me later instead of sooner. That if I do have feelings for him, it doesn't matter because I'll never be able to afford the kind of love that leads to a family, to children. And how can he? How can he after what we've just been through?

Try This:

With the next three novels you read, and the next three movies you watch, analyze the last fifty pages or the last ten minutes. First ask how you *feel* about the ending. What emotion is inside you?

Examine the emotion. Why do you feel it? What did the author or filmmaker do to make you feel that way? What specific parts of the craft were utilized?

Note, it's just as instructive to know why an ending fails to satisfy you as it is to know why it succeeds.

11

THE ENDING OF THIS BOOK ON ENDINGS

A guy brings a squirrel into a bar, and sets the cage down.

The bartender says, "What is that?"

The guy says, "A mystery writer."

"What? That looks like a squirrel."

"Yeah," the guy says. "He's a squirrel and he writes mysteries."

The bartender shakes his head. "Come on! How can a squirrel write a mystery?"

And the guy says, "Simple. He starts at the end and works his way back."

clears throat

But there's wisdom in the joke. If a squirrel can do it, you can.

Or maybe another bit of wisdom: knowing the end before you start will help your writing stay on a good track.

Remember, you can change your ending anytime. But at least something will be there for you to change.

And once you get to the end, write it for all it's worth. I spend more time on my last chapter than all the other parts of the book. It's not uncommon for me to revise the last page ten or twenty times. Not large-scale revisions or changes; it's mainly to get the sound right. I'll cut a word here or there, or add a line.

I'll read it out loud several times. I'm looking for the *Ah.* Maybe someday it'll be the *Uh-oh!*

Remember always that when a reader finishes your book, you want that reader to feel glad to know you, the writer. And anxious to read more of your work.

Katherine Anne Porter, winner of both the Pulitzer Prize and National Book Award, once said, "If I didn't know the ending of a story, I wouldn't begin. I always write my last lines, my last paragraph, my last page first, and then I go back and work towards it. I know where I'm going. I know what my goal is. And I know how I get there is God's grace."

All us writers need a little grace to get to the unforgettable endings we desire. I hope this book helps you find them.

AUTHOR'S NOTE

Thanks for reading my book. It's my great pleasure to help writers, so please take a moment to sign up for my occasional email updates. You'll be the first to know about my book releases and special deals. My emails are short and I won't stuff your mailbox, and you can certainly unsubscribe at any time.

You can sign up by going to the FREE BOOK page on my website:

www.jamesscottbell.com

Also, my comprehensive training course in the craft of bestselling fiction is now available. An investment that will pay off for your entire career.

https://knockoutfiction.teachable.com/p/novel

WRITING BOOKS BY JAMES SCOTT BELL

- Write Your Novel From The Middle
- Super Structure: The Key to Unleashing the Power of Story
- How to Write Dazzling Dialogue
- Plot & Structure
- Revision & Self-Editing
- Conflict & Suspense
- The Art of War for Writers
- Just Write
- How to Make a Living as a Writer
- Marketing for Writers Who Hate Marketing
- The Mental Game of Writing
- 27 Fiction Writing Blunders — And How Not to Make Them
- How to Write Short Stories, And Use Them to Further Your Writing Career
- How to Write Pulp Fiction
- Writing Fiction for All You're Worth
- Fiction Attack!

- Self-Publishing Attack!
- How to Write Comedy: The Danny Simon Notes

THRILLERS BY JAMES SCOTT BELL

The Mike Romeo Thriller Series

Romeo's Rules
Romeo's Way
Romeo's Hammer
Romeo's Fight

"Mike Romeo is a terrific hero. He's smart, tough as nails, and fun to hang out with. James Scott Bell is at the top of his game here. There'll be no sleeping till after the story is over."
- **John Gilstrap**, New York Times bestselling author of the Jonathan Grave thriller series

The Ty Buchanan Legal Thriller Series

Try Dying
Try Darkness
Try Fear

"Part Michael Connelly and part Raymond Chandler, Bell has an excellent ear for dialogue and makes contemporary L.A. come alive. Deftly plotted, flawlessly executed, and compulsively readable. Bell takes his place among the top authors in the crowded suspense genre." - **Sheldon Siegel**, *New York Times* bestselling author

Stand Alone Thrillers

Your Son is Alive
Blind Justice
Don't Leave Me
Final Witness
Framed

Zombie Legal Thrillers

You read that right. A new genre. Part John Grisham, part Raymond Chandler—it's just that the lawyer is dead. Mallory Caine, Zombie at Law, defends the creatures no other lawyer will touch…and longs to reclaim her real life.

Pay Me In Flesh
The Year of Eating Dangerously
I Ate The Sheriff

ABOUT THE AUTHOR

JAMES SCOTT BELL is a winner of the International Thriller Writers Award (*Romeo's Way)* and is the author of the #1 bestseller for writers, *Plot & Structure.* He studied writing with Raymond Carver at the University of California, Santa Barbara, and graduated with honors from the University of Southern California Law Center.

A former trial lawyer, Jim writes full time in his home town of Los Angeles.

For More Information

www.jamesscottbell.com

Printed in Great Britain
by Amazon

41444761R00066